Reaching Through
THE VEIL
of Deceit

Contents

DEDICATION 2
INTRODUCTION 3
PREFACE 4
FOREWORD 5
THE BEGINNING OF CHANGE 7
PLAYING WITH FIRE 19
SEPARATE LIVES 31
PLAYING HOUSE 41
DECEIVING SPIRITS 61
DARK DAYS 81
EXILED 105
NEW BEGINNINGS 131
DESPERATE SEARCHING 151
FALSE HOPES 183
THE UNVEILING 191
SET FREE 197
SPIRITS EXPOSED 211

Dedication

This book is dedicated to our four wonderful
children who have witnessed and supported us
through the many trials and tribulations
we have experienced as a family

To our close friends
and so many others over the years
we thank you for your love and loyalty
without which this book
could never have become a reality

We sincerely hope that reading about our
true life experiences will result in setting free
anyone who has been searching for the truth
in all the wrong places

Reaching through
THE VEIL
of deceit
INTRODUCTION

© 2010 Stan and Judy Rose

The contents of this book have been taken from actual events which we experienced as well as family members and friends during a period of time which created an insatiable appetite for the occult and the bizarre, all of which ultimately awakened the reality of the supernatural in ways that were to cause physical, emotional and financial challenges and suffering.

Long before this awakening however, dark spiritual forces became more and more brazen in their assignments of confusion, separation, fear and torment. An innocent experiment with the Ouija Board led us on a quest which ultimately led to so called psychic phenomenon, séances and a change of residence involving moving 3,600 miles to the west coast over the three great divides in hopes of escaping from these 'spirits', or, so we thought! Our newly acquired 'spiritual buddies' relentlessly followed every move and almost succeeded in causing a second divorce

For anyone reading this book, we advise you to think clearly before involving yourself in any form of spiritual connections claiming to know "the true power". It's an understatement that you will understand as you travel through these pages of time with us. Only our love and our search for real truth saved our marriage and also our very lives from a path which would have led to total destruction.

Reaching through
THE VEIL
of deceit
PREFACE

"Hey Jude, it's the spring of 2010. Whad'ya say we finally write the book we've been talking about for years?" "Right on Stan. We've been through a lot more than most people have experienced. If we divided up the years into time frames we could write a book on just those periods alone." "Yeah babe but I don't want to just get into all the lurid, sex-filled details that a lot of fiction novels have. Our life together has a much deeper meaning and purpose, especially in the supernatural don't you think?" "Stan, you know I wouldn't trade one minute of it for all the money in the world…..well….Okay, maybe some of it?" "Hey Jude, most Americans, don't have a clue to the reality of a spiritual existence. They think there are really ghosts…you know, like relatives visiting them after they died!" "Oh my gosh yes Stan, and how about Ouija boards, Psychics, Mediums, Witchcraft, New Age and all those other bizarre spiritual connections out there?" "Ya know babe, once we found out what the truth is, the truth set us free. I'd be dead or dying by now….maybe you too? I think the time has come to expose the 'spirits' for what they really are, don't you?" "Yes, and let's share the book. We'll write it together. Sometimes you talking, sometimes me". "Jude, we couldn't have done this years ago could we?" "Honey, the years have given us a lot of wisdom but especially a lot of patience with each other. So many people's lives have been messed up by The Veil of evil spirits…let's go

FOREWORD

I had hoped to sell all of my real estate holdings which were located 20 miles south of my home in deference to purchasing additional properties closer in so that I could attend an architectural college 40 miles north in an adjoining state. This would have given me the ability and time to manage my holdings more easily while pursuing a future in Architectural Design that I had long dreamed about. Although the sale w as made an I had begun my new education, my dream was crushed with two unexpected and unbelievable events. The man who purchased my two buildings on the main street of the quaint little village went bankrupt before the sale was complete. To make matters worse, the bank at closing had given him title without transferring the money to my account. So, in reality, he now owned the properties and could collect the rents and I was still responsible for the mortgages. At the same time, I was rushed to the hospital for an emergency gall bladder operation which disabled me for over a month.

"HEY ABE" I yelled into the phone from my private hospital room. "Sue that friggen Bank!....what the hell is going on here?"

"Listen Stan", Abe replied in his quiet non-reassuring manner, "The bank says it isn't responsible but, they have taken back ownership of the man's Real Estate building on the same block and they will return title of your other two buildings if you will agree to purchase his office building at 100% financing!" "WHAT?...damn it all...I guess I don't have a choice do I ? O.K., tell the bank I accept...no use going to court, they're a mafia controlled bank....they'd win in court that's for sure!" *So much for Architectural design,* I thought, as I hung up the phone in total anger and disgust.

As I steamed in thought about the impossible position I found myself in, I eventually believed that some unseen 'force' wanted me to stay in the quaint little town. Oh well, the new building is already a real estate office, and it even has an older guy in there who was the buyer's manager.

**I'll just keep him on and change the name on the sign.   ROSE REALTY...
hmmmm...it does have a nice ring to it!**

The beginning of change

Chapter 1

THE BEGINNING OF CHANGE

(Stan)

I woke up in the hospital room after my sudden gall bladder operation. It was later that day when my mother and wife came to visit me. As they entered the room they both looked like total strangers to me. In fact, my wife, in an attempt to please me had even had her hair styled completely differently which added to the confusion. I looked painfully at them and asked them to please just leave and go home. The date was Oct 19, 1972, the date of our ninth wedding anniversary. *Did something happen to me during the operation while under anesthesia?* I felt like someone I didn't know! By the following spring of 1973, I had totally recovered and had expanded my real estate ownership and brokerage with construction. My new partner Dennis shared my real estate office located in a one story building in the middle of a small seaside New England town where just about everyone knew everyone. Bankers included! Dennis and I had met a few years before when he remodeled one of my buildings next to my real estate office. By this time, I was the owner of almost one whole block in this quaint little town. It had two lanes running through it with just about any kind of store or restaurant a person could want and just about any kind of 'characters' owning the businesses including the customers. Dennis was married with four young children and I also had two young sons as well. We were both in our mid 30's and still very eager to sow some wild oats. I was a mild mannered Jewish kid; Dennis was a free spirited type guy of Portuguese descent. Together we seemed to make a good team, balancing each other's personalities as well as our new partnership in construction. I already had Harry, an older guy, as my Real Estate office manager but business was booming and we needed to hire an additional secretary to handle all the paperwork we hated to tackle.

SECRETARY WANTED
MUST BE YOUNG AND ATTRACTIVE

"Den! You can't possibly put that ad in the newspaper", I said in amazement.....we'll be sued for sure...are you crazy?" "NAH, Stan....you worry too much....watch what happens", Den replied with a smile that almost looked sinister. The parade of beautiful young hopefuls began. Every day seemed like we were judges in a beauty contest. They were all easy on the eyes, to say the least. One of them was even a former State Beauty Contest winner. "WOW, Den this is great....I thought you were nuts." Emotions within me were erupting that had submerged years before somewhere between my college days and my marriage. I couldn't quite get a grip on what was happening to me after all, I was a happily married man with two young children and a devoted wife. She was my childhood sweetheart. She was very pretty but also very conservative without any real definite opinions of her own. We had made a rather nice but kind of uneventful life together in the same community we grew up in along with many of the people we had always known. My business, however, was 20 miles south in the picturesque harbor side town I had always loved to visit. "HEY DEN, who's this coming into the office...she's awfully cute but why is she wearing that long trench coat? She's kind of pale...is that her skin color?...hmmmm, .she doesn't seem to be wearing any makeup either.....and her hair is pulled straight back..Oh well, let's see what she has to offer with her secretarial sklls.

"**SHE'S THE ONE**" !. Yelled Den. "Are you kidding", I replied. "Stan...she lives in the town, she knows all the business people here, she'll be a real asset in our combined businesses". "But Den...What about all those beauties who applied....I really liked a lot of them....especially the beauty queen!" As usual, I had become attuned to agreeing with my new partner and went along with his discernment. On the following morning, in walked Karen, the trench-coat lady. Hello? Her hair was hanging loose, blond and beautiful. She was wearing makeup and her rather perfectly shaped figure fit very sensually into her rather short mini-skirt, popularly stylish then during the early 70's. She knew who she was and went against all odds when she had first applied for the position. She figured that she would be hired for what she could do, not what she looked like. Den was smart and had seen right through the disguise. I wasn't that good of a judge of character when it came to the opposite sex so I went along kind of disappointed with my partner's choice of secretaries but I was, of course, not only surprised by her true appearance but she was also very sweet natured and hard working. She knew how to make an office efficient, that's for sure. She also captured Den's roving eyes as well. Weeks went by and our businesses continued to expand. Karen needed two weeks off for her family's summer vacation. "Hey Karen...do you have a friend or know someone who can fill in for you while you are gone", I asked. "Well I do have a close girlfriend but she's also married with children, like me and I'm afraid that with her responsibilities and working the three part-time jobs she already has, I don't think she'd do it...but I'll ask her anyway", Karen replied. That same evening Karen walked in with her friend Judy. She was wearing a mini-skirt topped by a blouse with puffy little shoulder length sleeves. Her pixie haircut and huge green eyes pierced right through the dim lighting.

(**Judy**)

"Let's clean up and close the Youth Center" Karen said. "How 'bout we run over to the Real Estate office where I work so I can introduce you to Mr. Rose?" "Well, okay. Karen, but just for a short time right?" We entered the office with only a desk lamp lighting the interior. I followed Karen closely behind her to the back of the room. She tried to introduce me to the man seated at a large executive desk but I kept moving side to side behind her as she turned in opposite directions wondering where I was. She and I laughed at how funny we both must have looked. The man looked fascinated as he chuckled along with us. "Hi Stan, this is Judy", Karen said half laughingly. "Hi Mr. Rose", I said as I tried to compose myself. "Please, just call me Stan, okay.?" he answered. "Okay Stan", I said, relieved to see that he saw the humor in it all. "Can I get you gals anything?" "Thanks but Karen and I just left the Youth Center so we're going to run down to the Harborside Tavern to relax for a while, maybe I can talk with you tomorrow about filling in for her, but I don't know if I can really manage the time. I'll have to give it some more thought. Gotta go now... see ya later!" Karen and I turned quickly back towards the door, still giggling over the awkward but funny introduction I had just experienced with Stan. Karen and I knew a lot of people in the Tavern by the bay. It was always a place where we could unwind before I would have to return home to my husband and two young children, all of them were usually sound asleep by then. Joe never wanted to communicate very much. I was a "people person" but he was not like that at all. He would never compliment me and I felt very insecure around him. I loved working part time at the Youth Center with Karen, I felt alive, especially having a part in helping teenagers who had no place else to go and no one to talk to. So many parents were too busy to bother looking into the distresses of the raging hormones and competition in these kid's school, their social lives and the need to express themselves. My children were only five and seven, still very young, so I felt I still had plenty of time to deal with them. I had lived, I thought, a good clean life, married, had children, stayed home but I knew there was more to life than that for me. Now here I was venturing out in to the world of teenage drugs and drinking. It sure does grow a person up quickly that's for sure. Joe just couldn't understand why I wanted to do this, on top of my other part time jobs. Kids were calling me at home even during late hours just to talk. I guess It made me feel needed and they were just reaching out. In a way, so was I. I always wanted to be a good wife and mom. I came from a divorced family and felt that marriage should be more sacred. A year before, I had found out that Joe was having an affair with my best friend. I never thought this would ever happen and it devastated me. Through it all though I still wanted to try and keep the marriage working but it was becoming very difficult.

(Stan)

"Hey Stan, Karen said Judy has a 'thing' for you"! "Yeah Den.... I have a THING for her all right!", I replied, hiding my true feelings and hoping he'd think that I was just referring to my newly awakened lustful ambitions. "This can't be happening", I thought. Den and I had joked a few times about getting a little action on the side. I had read books and articles and saw movies about these kinds of situations but I had always seen myself in a committed marriage, managing my business and family matters in a responsible upright manner. Who was I.? Or, more specifically, what was I becoming? Since my gallbladder operation the year before, I felt a change coming over me that I just couldn't understand. **"HEY POT-NA"**, yelled Denny from his back room office. It was a much larger room than the front office, but he needed it for all of his drafting tables and equipment. His pronunciation of the word "**partner**", coming mostly from his Massachusetts accent and his own unique way of speech permeated the air like an emergency vehicle on the street. "Yeah! now what"? I answered in my typically suspicious way. Every time Denny spoke up like that, it meant he had some new situation or project in mind. Although I was getting used to it, I was still not quite comfortable with my normal business routine being interrupted this way but he did inject a measure of excitement which I found irresistible to deny. I was still dressed every day in what I thought was proper business attire. Denny, however, sat comfortably in a strange combination of loose pullover shirts, wrinkled pants and funny shoes. He even managed to trim his own hair sometimes by putting a bowl over his head! I always hoped he would stay in his back room office when Real Estate clients walked in, but of course, this was almost never the case. "SAN LOOK!", he yelled....what a beauty! Den was now even calling me by his own nickname. By this time I was answering to anything that even sounded like my name. I thought he was going to show me another girlie photo but to my amazement it was a picture of a ten yr old, 38 foot, twin engine Chris Craft Yacht for sale, complete with fly bridge, lower galley and twin births at the unbelievable price of only $12,000. "Let's buy it", he said. A certain tone of his voice indicated to me he was very serious, no joking this time. "You've got to be kidding", I answered. "How does that fit into our business plans and why do we need anything like that?" "Look San, the property we own together has enough income to pay for it and besides we can entertain our business prospects and Bankers on it. Hey, don't forget, we can drive it over to the Harborside Tavern and we can invite Karen and Judy on board if they are there!" His remarks bounced around in my head like a pinball machine but for some strange reason I thought the prospect of owning a yacht would be another "notch" of personal success in my belt notwithstanding the thought of entertaining clients and such. I still couldn't quite understand what was happening to my practical business thinking and for some strange reason I didn't quite care. "All right Den, let's go look at it. Does it have a name?" "Yeah San it's called UTOPIA". "Doesn't that mean ultimate perfection or something like that?" I said in a muffled voice. "I dunno" Denny said, "who cares? It looks great, we should buy it!" By Memorial Day we were the proud owners of an impressive Cabin Cruiser. We hired a captain to drive us up the coast to our birth near the Harborside Tavern We had also invited Karen and Judy to join us on our maiden voyage with booze available in our downstairs fridge. Being right behind Judy when she climbed up the stairs to the deck of the yacht that day, I was staring right at her shapely buns, easily in view underneath her rather short mini skirt. "Boy, I'd better not inform my wife about buying the yacht just yet", I thought. She was already noticing a change in my behavior at home. **BANG! ...what was that?** Our Captain had misjudged the direction of the boat in the bay and it hit a large submerged rock which destroyed the struts and the propellers. This whole new situation really had me very nervous, but somehow it was exciting and I knew Denny would somehow get us out of it. Unlike me, he always kept his cool. We managed to contact Karen's husband who was employed by the Fire Department in our town. He got us off the boat and onto land. The Utopia was towed back to the Marina for repairs where we had purchased it and where we had just left that very day for our first trip out. They could hardly believe what had happened. Denny and I had just completed a week long navigational course only a few days before. "OY VEY"! the typical Jewish response to perplexing situations had entered my thoughts more than once since becoming partners with Denny but then, the more time I was spending around Judy, the less I cared about much of anything or anyone else. She had an unbeatable smile and she had a way of being trusted by total strangers. She actually knew no strangers....only friends she hadn't met. Her large crab-like green eyes, her pixie haircut and her slightly freckled skin turned me on as I had never been turned on before. She was slightly built but she had legs which wouldn't quit....like a showgirl in Vegas. "I'd better stop looking at her the way I have been lately", I thought. Although my wife had a cute figure, there was no comparison. Judy was a total 'package deal' with a personality to boot. I tried to hide my emotions but there seemed to be this 'force' driving me. I knew it wasn't just normal; it was something else. (**like a stranger living inside me**) Since I had recently discovered TM (Transcendental Meditation), I attended local meetings where I was given a personal "Mantra" for meditation. Sessions lasted sometimes for 2 hrs but seemed like minutes. My new life was beginning to test my ability to handle multi-tasking much less the double life I was leading. The office was becoming a very busy place that summer of 1973. Judy had decided to fill in as many hours as she could. She had even quit one of her three part time jobs in town to assist her friend Karen and us helpless males as well. By then, we had strange 'fellows' working for us in our construction business. One was a plumber by the name of Sneezik and another was his sleazy helper who kept hanging around Judy's desk hoping for a date. That was it!. "O.K. pal", I said loudly, "hands off the secretary....got it?" I couldn't believe I reacted that way. It wasn't my nature but it sure felt good! "Umm...Judy...how ja like to go for a lunch break down the block at the diner?" "O.K. Stan", she answered, "just give me a few more minutes to get these files put away". "How ja?" Oh my God, I'm even starting to talk like Denny. As we walked down the block it felt like nothing I had ever felt before. She was so much fun to be around. Our lunch break turned out to be two hours long. I was hanging around her desk so much she hardly had time to complete the paperwork I was feeding her. I would actually find any reason to bother her, and she was very aware by now that I was doing just that. Karen was away on vacation and Den kept himself out of sight in the back room a lot. I could tell that he was really missing Karen's presence a lot.

"**HEY SAN!**" The familiar voice from the back office pulled me away from Judy's desk abruptly. "**WHAT?**", I yelled back. "Know what San?, I'm gonna get me a Honda 950. Why doan you get you one too?" The thought of it scared me almost as much as buying the yacht but within a week, we were ridin' buddies, Den was real confident on his 950....me, a lot less sure on a slightly smaller 450, but hey, my life was changing by the week. "Buying a bike took care of my "business" attire", that's for sure I thought. Jeans weren't in full fashion yet, but durable pants and a helmet gave me a total new look. By mid summer if Judy wasn't working in the office, I'd be meeting her in the town near where she worked one of her part time jobs. I'd bring a lunch and we'd just sit on a short stone wall and talk during whatever time she could take. It was getting to the point that I almost couldn't stand not being around her and it was very obvious that she felt the same way. Even though her husband Joe knew a lot of town folks, we didn't care at all who knew what. In fact, Joe was friends with Karen's husband so it was only a matter of time before the 'fit hit the shan' so-to-speak! "Hey beautiful", I asked as I stared into Judy's large green eyes... "could we get together for a drink tonight at the Harborside?" "Well, Okay, but I can't stay too long. Joe is getting a little upset at my late hours. I need to be getting home a little earlier at night, especially for my kids too. She sounded excited and nervous at the same time and the thought of maybe even getting to do a slow dance with her got my heart beating so loud I thought she could hear it. "K", see ya then Stan".

I never saw time pass as slowly as it did that day until we met later on.

PLAYING WITH FIRE

(Judy)

"Karen, guess what I did today?....I bought a bikini, I never wore one, I don't know what Joe will say but I don't care"! "Look Judy, wear it tomorrow O.K.? and let's go to Garner Park for a swim", Karen's instant suggestion shocked me to the reality of what I just told her but I agreed. There was a small beach at the lake and there weren't very many people on it in the middle of the week anyway. As I was trying on my new look in swimwear, Joe walked in. "What are you wearing? You're not serious about going out in public like that are you? Cover up"! Joe's voice and face said it all. I never argued with him and I had always been quite intimidated by him, so I just kept quiet. For years he made me feel insecure, wear turtlenecks to hide my long neck and he also wanted me to get a breast implant, but I drew the line from his insistence about that. I did resort to stuffing my bras to make me look like I had larger breasts just to please him but somehow I was never that uncomfortable with my 5'4" height, 115lbs and smaller boobs.

The next day found me and my kids at Garner Park wearing my new bikini. I felt truly pretty for the first time. Karen always wore them and she always looked great. To my surprise I turned around towards the parking area and saw this burgundy colored Buick Riviera drive up. There was only one person in the whole town who owned that car, it was Stan. **"Karen....Stan's here!"** I wondered if the whole beach heard me. How'd he know we were here? "OK. Judy" Karen responded with a smirk, "I stopped by the office; they asked me where you were since it was your day off so I told them. You know Judy; I think Stan really likes you". "Karen, he is so attractive but I'm really trying to get my life back on track with Joe". "Right, Judy I have to go now....have fun". I was very nervous. I liked Stan a lot but I was afraid of just how much. Before I knew it, I watched Karen disappear and Stan appearing almost on top of the blanket I was laying on. "Judy, Karen thought I should come by and say hi". ("great line" I thought, "but I was excited that he did, especially with me wearing my new bikini"). "Stan, these are my children, Kurt, he's seven and Holly, she's six". "Hello Mr. Rose". "Holly, you can just call me Stan, OK.?" "OK. Stan". As they ran off to go swimming Stan sat down on the blanket. Running his finger up my faded appendix scar he said..."So Judy, what have you been doing since your operation?" I giggled nervously at his words and the sight of me in a bikini and him all dressed up on the beach. It all struck me funny. After a time of small talk, Stan jumped up. "I have to go back to the office, see ya tomorrow", he said as he walked towards his car without taking his eyes off me. On the way home, I couldn't wait for tomorrow to happen. Every bit of excitement was bubbling up out of me. I felt pretty and special. Uh oh, I thought, this could turn into an affair. I had a few before just to spite Joe because of his fling with my best friend. Well, I thought she was my best friend until I found out about it. I hadn't been brought up like this. I was always a good girl and a virgin when I got married but *something hit me* when I turned 30. I felt a change coming over me that I couldn't ignore and didn't want to. I just couldn't seem to turn off the excitement within. I was on my way to change alright...***like a veil*** that covered right from wrong. But I could not deny my heart. So many of us judge others but we never know the whole story behind the life of the person we are criticizing. Mine was based on my childhood filled with fear and anxieties. A stepfather who put me in a dark basement if I didn't eat my dinner or the fat on the meat. A mother who yelled and swatted me and my brothers a lot was causing me to hide out in closets. We all have secrets and I definitely wanted out of the closet. The excitement I was feeling working in the office around Stan and Denny and all their strange friends is exactly what I needed to do just that! Stan and I began to meet for lunch, a drink after work then dancing at the Harborside after I closed up the Youth Center. I was falling in love and I knew it. We wound up spending hours on his yacht Utopia....and 'UTOPIA' it was. "Stan", I said in a whisper, "there's a man on the dock and he's taking pictures of the boat. "Uh oh" Stan said with a half smile on his face, "I think your hubby or my wife has hired a P.I."! From that time on everywhere we went there he was! One night we crawled on the office floor so he wouldn't see us but, after a while, we just didn't care. The day came when we decided to just tell our spouses. But first I wanted to spend some time with my mother. Even though we had our problems together she was still my mother and I really needed her advice.

"Mom, I've tried to work on my marriage but every time I think of Joe and giving up Stan, I feel so empty. When Joe had the affair, I thought I had forgiven him but I guess I closed the door and searched for love through others". "Judy, Stan has a lot of money and has showered you with luxuries you haven't been used to but ask yourself if he lost it all would you still love him?" WOW! I really had to think about her words. As I walked around getting my thoughts together, I felt an unusual discomfort and made a sudden trip to the bathroom. Barely entering it I felt myself doubling over in pain. Oh my gosh, the cramps became very intense and I couldn't move for a second and when I did I realized that something was seriously wrong. "MOM!" I screamed. My mom came running in. "What's wrong?" I began to cry. "LOOK!". "Oh dear...Judy, did you know?" "No mom, I had no idea I was pregnant." "How old do you think the baby is?" "Probably about two months, I guess. Mom, that's Stan's and my baby!" The fetus just dropped out. My mom calmed me down and I realized it was probably for the best. My mom was so understanding that weekend and I was glad that I was able to be with her then. "Mom, I have thought about it. Yes, I love Stan unconditionally and now I know it's not just the money". Boy, what a true statement that was going to be.

LET THE GAMES BEGIN!

Stan moved to the back room of the office building along with Den who had also separated from his wife. Stan was quite distraught and so was I. Joe knew something was going on and showed up one night at the Harborside with a gun thinking I was dating Denny because we were good friends and together a lot. Karen warned me and Stan and went out and spoke to Joe. He decided to just go home but I became very fearful. I had two beautiful children and so did Stan....what in the world were we doing? Our love had become very deep and that's all we knew. I tried to break it off and Stan thought about going back to his wife but, after all, we had gotten to this point because we just weren't happy. Joe and I talked. He cried and wanted me back. "Oh Joe, in nine years you never told me how you felt, showed compassion or made me feel good about myself. It may be too late. I have to get out of here, I'm going to go to New Jersey and stay with Carol". Although she had been my best friend and the girl Joe had an affair with behind my back, it somehow still made good sense to me to stay with her. "Are you crazy?" he said, I nodded yes. I still considered her my friend. (*deceived again!*). I cried a lot until I got to New Jersey. Carol welcomed me and told me how sorry she was about what happened and somehow I understood as we sat and talked for hours.

(Stan)

"She went where?" I yelled over the phone to Den. I was on my way back to the office and had stopped at a convenience store for another pack of cigarettes after another uncomfortable meeting with my wife that morning. I had given up smokes for a few years but by now I had started smoking more than ever. "Den, tell Harry to take over any office business for a few days, I'm flyin' out to Jersey as soon as I can get a ticket". It was a short ride from the store to the airport and, as luck would have it, there was a flight to LaGuardia Airport in New York leaving within an hour. I hadn't packed anything and I didn't care. Whatever I would need I could buy. My pulse was racing as the plane landed. I had no time to bother renting a car so I jumped into a cab and told the driver to take me over the river to the nearby town in New Jersey where Judy was staying. He joked in his funny New York accent "Hey buddy, it'll cost ya 40 bucks! Ya know that?". Before leaving the airport, I was able to get Karen to call Judy and tell her I was on my way and for her to pick me up. The cab cost me more than the plane fare to New York, but I could have cared less. I knew what was going on in Judy's head and I couldn't bear the thought of losing her back to Joe. Arriving at the pre determined pick up spot I met the duo. "So, this was the infamous Carol that Judy talked about?" I thought. Standing next to Judy she was obviously bigger busted and a little taller (typically what Judy's husband might have preferred) but I quickly focused back on Judy. She looked totally amazed at my presence there. I could hardly take my eyes off her. After a short visit to Carol's home, I insisted that Judy and I spend the rest of the weekend in Manhattan. There we were, in two adjoining phone booths on the corner in the middle of New York City talking to our spouses, telling them that we were doing some serious thinking about our marriages while all the time looking at each other through the clear glass surrounding us. Nothing made any sense to us at all except being together. Judy hadn't really brought much clothing with her so I took her to the nearest women's store and bought her a cute little printed silk dress for the evening. After dinner we went to a Broadway musical, her very first. I spent most of the time just staring at her. Her big eyes were glued at the stage during the entire performance. That night at a posh hotel in the Theatre district proved to be a time of intimacy and ecstasy that literally felt like we caused the whole building to shake! Since Judy had driven to New Jersey we returned home in her car the next day and spent the whole drive home trying to figure out what our next move should be. There was no turning back now and no way that we could ever be totally apart from each other again.

(Judy)

Carol and I had cleared the air about why everything had happened. I guess I was always a forgiving person or just plain naïve. "STAN! what are you doing in Jersey?" I still couldn't believe he had followed me, but my heart skipped a beat at the sound of his voice. "I just couldn't let you go Judy but right now I need you to come get me". As Carol and I raced to pick Stan up I wondered how I was going to work this all out. Here I am trying to make some decisions on my marriage but I know as soon as I see him, I'm done. I love Stan. Oh my, there he is, my heart began to race. I ran to hug him like never before. We drove back to Carol's house and after a short visit we decided to go to New York City for a few days. At the same time, we called our spouses from side to side phone booths asking them for more time and to be patient. (the VEIL of deception grew deeper). Is this what love does? I hated not telling the truth, but I just couldn't, not now! Stan showered me with a beautiful silk dress and my very first pair of clunky platform shoes. They were so high I had to hold on to him to walk right. He took me to my first Broadway musical and a night in a five star hotel which could only be related to a fantasy come true! As we drove back home the following day, we were both very frightened to tell our spouses that it was all over. I was in tears most of trip but I didn't want to let go of the love I finally found so deep after 32yrs. As I walked through my front door, Joe was waiting with flowers; a sign was hung with welcome home on it. The kids were dancing and giggling because mommy was home. He hugged me but felt my resistance. "I guess you've made your decision right?" "Joe, let's sit down and talk please?" "I want an answer now....what is it?" His voice changed from a happy expectation to the stern level I was used to dealing with over the years. I began to cry. I'm sorry Joe, I tried but I just can't come back to you!" Everything changed from that moment on. Joe became increasingly distant and angry. That evening I slept on the couch and for the following four or five months that became my bed.

The following day there was a huge rose on my desk from Stan. "Hi Judy, how'd it go?" I just put my hand up with tears in my eyes. "What about you, Stan?" "Well, right now, I just decided to move all my clothes and things into the office backroom. Joyce was totally hurt. She kept yelling "I've failed" and threw her wedding ring across the room. I almost couldn't stand the reality of it all myself." Stan and I were both very quiet the rest of the day. We didn't want to hurt anyone but we were fooling ourselves. There would be plenty of hurt to come, that's for sure. A few weeks went by and one day a car pulled up with Sherriff marked on it. The man got out and headed right for the office. "I'm looking for Judy Charney" he said very loudly. "That's me" I responded. Still not quite sure of what was happening, I opened the paperwork and discovered it was a legal divorce document. I didn't have the money to file so Joe had done it first. Stan tried to convince me to protect myself and pull most of the money out of the bank and hire an attorney but Joe held all the accounts. "I can't do that Stan". "Ok Judy, then I will hire a lawyer for you. If you don't have one, you'll be totally unprotected" To this day I cannot believe how naïve I was, I really was, I knew nothing about the law. I still lived with Joe but we never talked much. I had nowhere else to go and I was determined not to lose my children. I never wanted this. It all started with Joe's affair then mine. There was a greater force at work here. Deception had crept in like a veil and there was no way out. Finally, after six months I decided to move out of my beautiful home on a cul de sac. Denny and Stan tried in vain to convince me to stay with my children and force Joe out. I tried but he wouldn't budge. I found a nice apartment on a third floor. It was part of HUD which I could afford and it was still in a very nice area of town. I was on my way to a new life totally on my own. Locating sitters for my kids was difficult and even those I found I later discovered that they were using drugs. I worked hard just to pay for food and rent but I had to do it on my own. Stan had a lot of money and even offered to pay my rent but I wanted to be independent.

As time went on, Dennis met Jackie, a beautiful red head at the Harborside. She was tall, snappy and very funny. They were a perfect couple. Our curiosity about knowing the future was discussed especially during times of partying and "tripping out" on some really good marijuana. Stan and Den had begun to purchase whole 'bricks' of the stuff so that they could sell most of it and enjoy the rest at no cost to themselves so there was always an ample supply on hand. "**Hey you guys**", it was Skeezix, the company plumber's voice on the office intercom. "Yeah Skeezix", we all answered in unison, hardly able to contain our laughter. Skeezix was really good at his work but he was a real funny dude in his appearance and sense of humor, which made us all laugh a lot even when we were completely sober. "**O.K**.!" he yelled over the phone, cut the laughing, I got something important to tell you. I just met this gal who's a Psychic. I told her all about you guys and she says you should make an appointment and see her right away. "**A Psychic**?" Jackie screamed. "What the frig is she?...some kind of sooth sayer? She gonna tell me what my great grandmother ate for breakfast ...or what?" "Hey look you guys, get serious, this gal seemed very concerned about you". "Ok Skeezix, calm down, give me her number, I'll call her later", Stan replied, hardly containing the laughter still evident in his voice. "NOT LATER, CALL HER NOW she's waiting for you, says she can see you all this morning!" Skeezix's voice sounded more firm than we had ever heard before so we composed ourselves, that is, Stan composed himself and made the call. Upon arriving, the cottage style house looked harmless enough and although we were still a little high and joking about the meeting, we started to get a little apprehensive about whatever this strange woman had to say to us. We were all greeted by an older lady dressed kind of frumpy. Her furniture and décor looked like something that time had passed by. We were then called into another room where she proceeded to tell us of all the happiness and prosperity that she saw in our future along with a few dangers we should be aware of. Stan and I were planning a short weekend bike trip to the shore areas on a particular highway. The lady advised against the trip altogether but if we insisted on going, at least not to go on that highway.

"Whad'ya think about the Psychic?" I asked as we got back in the car. "Who cares", shouted Denny, "Let's party some more, I think she's a real crackpot". "Did you see the inside of that house?" Jackie said with her cynical laughter, "what the frig was she wearing? and the house smelled like a cat died or somethin, get me outa here...NOW"! As we drove away, I couldn't help remembering that the woman had told me about my life ending at a certain age, (words that would haunt and terrify me for years but which would be totally false by the end of this book). That and the bike trip had me a little on edge for the rest of the day and I wasn't completely able to rejoin the fun we were having earlier. When it came time for our bike trip, I insisted that Stan take a different route which we did and nothing of any danger harmed us. The meeting with that so-called "Psychic" left an uneasy feeling within me. Stan was concerned enough to change travel plans but Jack and Den shrugged it all off as nonsense. It was the beginning however, of an inquisitive search for the 'un-known' for Stan and myself which would draw us deeper and deeper into a spirit realm determined to destroy us in any way it could.

(***the Veil of deceit had been drawn tighter***)

The four of us went everywhere together. By New Year's Eve we went to a New Hampshire resort. "Stan! Look!...it's the lawyer I hired, what in the world is he doing here?". I couldn't believe my eyes. Here we were, hundreds of miles from home on a dance floor and my affair with Stan now in full view of my defense attorney! By March of the next year we were still living in our own make believe world. **"JUDE!"** It was Stan on the phone. His voice was sad and quivered. "My mother passed away, they are saying it's a suicide...too many sleeping pills! I had just stopped by her house to see her but as I entered, I heard her snoring loudly so I left quietly. I felt good that she was finally sleeping because she had been so upset over my separation from Joyce. She had even been blaming herself for interfering in our marriage. When I got back to her house my whole family was there ahead of me ransacking the place and blaming me for killing her! Jude, honey, if I don't call you for a while please understand. I have to set up the funeral and Jews grieve for one week. It's called "sitting Shiva" After I hung up the phone, I whispered to myself "goodbye my beautiful Stan". I knew how close he was with his mother and he would blame himself for her death. When I finally did see him, he wasn't the same loveable man I met. He was very distant with me. I tried to be patient and understand but couldn't stand the separation and lack of attention I had grown to love from him. Every time we made love, Stan was rough and snappy. "Who is this man? Have I lost that compassionate guy I fell in love with?" Stan became more and more distant from me and decided to take a break from our relationship for a while, the pain, guilt and grief from the loss of his mother was too much for him to deal with. I also couldn't handle the pain of losing him. After putting the children to bed one night I grabbed a bottle of wine and a few pills to relax the torment raging inside me and the next thing I heard was my phone ringing next to me where I had passed out. "HELLO, JUDY IT'S BEN, what's wrong, talk to me!...did you take pills? liquor?" Ben was so sweet; he knew by the way I was slurring my words that something was seriously wrong. Ben was a friend who had helped me out after I found out that my husband Joe was having an affair. He was there to pick up the pieces after my shocking discovery of it.

I liked Ben a lot and after a while we had also gotten together intimately but we ended it very quickly, remained friends and I told him to go back to his wife. He kept me on the phone a long time until he was sure I was alright. That was the first affair I ever had and only the second man I had ever made love to. I was so upset, I took a week off from my jobs and with some money I had saved, flew to Miami, Florida with my children and stayed with my cousin in her home there. She was actually a lot older than me and I always regarded her as my aunt. I managed to contact some friends from my old high school that I attended and just hid myself at parties for a while. We were all well taken care of and having a deserved rest and fun in the sun. I was always a 'sun' person, hating cloudy damp weather and loved the refreshing difference from the lingering winter.

Separate Lives

Chapter 3

SEPARATE LIVES

"Judy darling", my aunt said as she walked into my room and handed me a letter which was in her mailbox. "I think it's from Stan". "Oh Babs, should I open it? I'm so nervous!" "You'll always wonder if you don't", she answered. I could hardly believe what I was reading.

"Dear Judy. I must say, I miss you a lot but I need some time alone. This has been so hard on me and I feel we need a break in our relationship. I've been going out a lot and seeing others but I would rather tell you instead of you hearing it from someone else. Your friend Myra spent a fun day with Denny and me and then she came back to my apartment and slept over. It didn't mean anything to me but it happened."

My best friend again! I threw the letter in a ball across the room and burst into tears. Babs sat with me while I poured my heart out. Why is it that all the men I like, sleep with my best friends? Joe even made advances to Karen, but she wouldn't have anything to do with him. Well, at least that was one consolation. But the hurt was almost too much for me to take from Stan. That night I went to a party with my friends as sunburned as I was from the beach where I drowned my sorrows for most of that day. Nothing was making any sense to me anymore. The week passed and we arrived back home looking like lobsters. I felt really bad for Kurt and Holly; they were really burnt from the hot Florida sun. Funny thing about love, I still hoped I would see Stan at the airport but only Karen was there to drive us home. The next day I dressed up really cute and decided to go to the office to see Dennis. Dennis and I chatted for a while and then Stan walked in. He wanted to talk but I couldn't deal with our new relationship so I left as quickly as I had arrived. That evening I went to the Harborside with some friends. As usual, Stan and Dennis were there with the yacht docked nearby. I tried dancing with other men just to push myself away from him but it all seemed like a nightmare. Life was so different now. I had lived with my parents, got married, had

32

children and here I was single again, living in my own apartment. I never had this kind of independence. It was all very new and refreshing but it was also very frightening. "Fred, do you think you could take me home?" Fred was Jackie's brother so I felt comfortable around him. "You can come on up and see my new apartment if you want to". Fred was so sweet and I was so vulnerable. He was still single, we were both lonely, and wound up making love. The next morning the guilt began and I realized how much I was hurting. Since I've been little I was always promised things but never received the promises. Stan promised but hurt me instead. Deception was following me everywhere I went it seemed. I guess I expected it to happen so I realized I must somehow be attracting it! I loved Stan but I knew I couldn't have him so I quit working for him and got a full time job on a switchboard. I had two children to support and that had to be my focus from now on.

"I'm looking for Judy Charney" It was that same Sherriff asking for me again. I couldn't imagine what this visit was all about. He handed me the papers. Alienation of Affection? Another legal doc from Joe. What does that mean? I called Karen and she explained it to me. It was a copy of a law suit sent to Stan. Joe was suing Stan for a quarter of a million dollars for causing our divorce. This was hard for me to comprehend. These legal terms were over my head. I never had any dealings with lawyers or courts. I called my divorce lawyer but he wasn't any help at all so I fired him. From the talk we had that day, I believed he was actually in cahoots with Joe's lawyer. I didn't trust him at all. He hadn't really helped me to get any settlement. I even wondered how he had suddenly appeared at the same resort we were at during my New Year's trip. Like Stan always said, it didn't look "Kosher" at all! Joe was due to receive more profit from the house and car. I wound up with my little VW which needed a push to it get started sometimes. Guilt had stopped me from fighting.

Well, the day came that Joe and I had to sign off on our home after we sold it. I had no legal representation at that time. I was furious with Joe at what he and his lawyer were trying to do to Stan so I called them both into a private room. "O.K., look I'm not signing anything today." "What? What do you mean Judy, You have to" stammered Joe's lawyer. "Oh no I don't" I replied firmly. "You can go to jail if you don't" argued Joe in a menacing tone. "So....I'll get free room and board!" I was so angry and scared at the same time I felt myself shaking and hoping they wouldn't notice. Even though Stan and I had broken up I couldn't let them do that to him. I looked them both in their face and repeated myself again. "Unless you drop the law suit against Stan, I will not sign!" "JUDY, Joe begged, be reasonable, we can split the money!" Look Joe, one last time, tell the people to go home, I am not signing the house over today. At my last insistence, Joe and his lawyer looked at each other and said "Okay., you win". "Oh no you don't, I want it all in writing or I'm leaving right now!" They agreed, the house was sold and Stan was free and clear of any law suit. WOW! I was proud of myself. This was a big move for me. I finally stood up for my rights. In the past I had always backed off of any confrontation due to my fear of authority.

(Stan)

"Hi Judy", it was Stan's voice on the phone. "Thank you hon, I received the papers releasing the law suit. I heard all about what you did from Karen. That must have been awfully hard for you. You are something else babe, I can't thank you enough and I am so proud of you"

"**HEY DEN!**" "Yeah potna, what's up?" Den yelled back from his office". "I got a friend coming here soon to give us some financial advice. His name is Smitty. He's a true Leprechaun Irishman; wait 'till you meet this guy. "Who'd you say San? He's a what? Denny yelled back. I never knew whether he had actually heard me or whether he was just too busy or what, but he drove me a little nuts when he responded that way. I started to walk back to Den's office when I heard the front door open. Low and behold, the Irishman came strolling in. I had met Smitty during a real estate purchase I was making a year before. He was the go-between-the-Bank and me, kind of a loan-aranger. In fact, that was my favorite name for him but I combined the name to 'The Lone Ranger' like the old movie star. He sometimes seemed to appear and disappear at will. Now you see him, now you don't, just like a fairytale Leprechaun. "HEY, QUE PASA Senor", he blurted. (Smitty always greeted everyone in Spanish which made him even more of a character I thought), "Hi Smitty, long time no see, come on back and meet my potna". "POTNA?" said Smitty, "what kind of word is that? "Hey, its short for partner...this is him right here, that's the way he talks. You and he ought-a get along great. I've been hanging around him too long; I'm even starting to talk like him." "SO, I hear you and San know each other for a while huh?", Den said as he jerked his head quickly off the drafting table. I could tell they hit it off instantly. The three of us became the three "musketeers" in very short order. Smitty loved to party and so did we. and he started to visit us more and more often after his first visit. In fact, our end of the day partying had begun earlier and earlier. At first, from 5pm to 3pm, finally noon and then sometimes all day. Our work schedule got very sloppy with Judy and Karen not at the job of keeping the office professional. Smitty had found out that we also liked to smoke a little weed now and then and he became our closest source of supply. My faithful Real Estate office manager Harry always came in early and cleaned up all the beer cans and mess we had made the night before. He was retired and didn't even want a paycheck, but I treated him well. Our Honda 950 and 450 bikes, helmets and all had taken place of the secretarial desk in the front lobby. I sure had come a long way from my respectable past. During the months since my mother had passed and Judy and I had split, I dated just about any gal I could, including our Interior Designer and a gal biker I met at a club. My life had become one big empty pit that I tried to fill with booze, drugs and girls. The only stable thing in my life were my two little boys, Steve and Elliot and, to some extent, my real estate holdings which I had been neglecting a lot. The Real Estate market had also been slipping due to a sliding economy during President Carter's time of office. We found ourselves in gas lines and worse; our current President Nixon was about to close the Naval Base close by which I depended a lot on to fill my apartments with tenants. But, the partying increased and, as 'they say' (whoever 'they' are?) "Que sera sera"! I missed my Judy and I woke up one day and asked myself the one question I hadn't asked. "Who do you really love?"

Did I still want to go back to my past? Did I still want to return to my wife and boys? The answer came fast. I could not deny my heart. There was only one name which rang clearly that morning. It was JUDY! I missed her keen sense of humor, her looks, her intelligence and everything about her.

(Judy)

It was a beautiful summer day. I had just returned home from work looking forward to the weekend and there was a knock on the door. **"STAN"**, what are you doing here? He took me by complete surprise and I could do nothing more than to want to give him a big hug, but I tried to act calm and cool. "Come with me babe", he said. The children were with Joe and I hesitated, but I was, after all, free. "Where are we going?" I asked, questioning his intentions. "Big surprise, that's all I can tell you", Stan said. Stan had traded his Buick for a brand new Ford T-Bird. It was all white outside, and white leather inside. I thought I was in a limo as we drove quietly several miles out of town on a gorgeous country road called Frenchtown Lane that I was familiar with. It was the road that the elementary school my children used to go to was on. As we rounded a small dip in the road, Stan pulled into a long winding dirt driveway past two short stone pillars. The hard dirt surface curved around a picture postcard white colonial house with stone walls and hedges. In front of the house was a cobblestone parking area complete with an old hitching post. The scene was breathtaking with huge trees surrounding it on all sides. It was very old but it also looked new at the same time. "What a beautiful home, who lives here and who lives in that house in the back? And that Barn and Carriage house wow!", gosh what a sight it was! I could hardly take it all in. "Oh, a few single guys live in the back house, you'll see…just wait." Stan answered with a chuckle and a smile I hadn't seen for a long time. I thought he was stopping to get a closer look at some real estate deal he was working on. As we got out of the car, he opened the back door and we went inside. To my surprise, the house was completely empty. It looked like the house in the movie The Great Gatsby to me. My eyes got so big. A huge living room opened into the sunroom through French doors on either side of the double fireplace. The kitchen was old but updated. Up the stairs we went to view the four bedrooms and a bath which had an old fashioned claw foot tub. Stan said the house was about 150 years old and sat on over four acres and it also backed up to ten more. It was on the historic records of the town as well. As I looked around thinking how nice it would be to live in it Stan said, "Do you like it?" "Like it? Who wouldn't like it? I gasped. It's so big and look at all the land. There's even a pond across the road in the front of it. It's a dream home!" Stan looked at me with a love in his eyes which I hadn't seen or felt in months. "Well hon, how would you like to really live here? I rented it today" "WHAT" I said, totally surprised by his remark, we were not even going together and he's asking me to live here? "What do you mean Stan?" "Well Judy, I've done of lot of thinking and I know I will have two more children to help raise but I love you and I can't lose you". "Stan, are you sure? You know that my kids are my world. That's a big step for you but if we do live together your boys will be my world too. I know they can't be with us every day but I would like them to be here as much as possible". Our kids had already been introduced to each other in the past. This would be a fantastic place for them to play together in safety. I jumped up and down, racing all over the house. "YES, YES, YES" That's all I could say. As we looked around at the house wondering what it would be like living here together, we made love to celebrate our new union.

(Stan)

O.K., I thought, the die is cast, no going back now. The bank I was dealing with, through my newly acquired friend, marijuana supplier and financial counselor Smitty, had called me to see if I might be interested in owning a home which they had foreclosed on with beautiful acreage on the outskirts of the town. The price of only $75,000 in 1975 at 100% financing was tempting, but the real estate market had been falling and unstable for the past several months and my own holdings were in deep trouble. The bank which held the mortgage on the historic Colonial home also held the mortgage on my real estate office building in town. All four major banks in the State were also the mortgage holders of several other properties I owned and they as well as the bank that owned the colonial house, didn't know that I was quickly heading for bankruptcy. I hardly believed it myself. Over a year had gone by since my mother's passing and the economy was still in a nose dive with banks calling in notes I owed for construction as well as unplanned vacancies popping up in my real estate holdings everywhere. The stock market had plunged to extremely low levels and percentages of construction loans backed up by blue chip stocks I owned were being called in almost weekly. Thousands of dollars were drained weekly from my business accounts. Two homes which Den and I had built also hadn't sold and finally we had to settle for sales with very little profit. As if all of this weren't enough to worry about, there was also a major possibility of my wife filing for divorce proceedings. So I had opted instead to offer the bank a rental situation which they had agreed to.

WHOA! As I walked up to the house through high uncut grass, something brushed by my leg at super speed. It shocked me at first then I realized it was only a friendly Doberman/Shepherd puppy that lived in the servant's house out back. I found out later, that her name was Sha-bam, named after gunfire. She would also become a permanent part of my newly acquired family. The days grew shorter for Judy and me to move into the house. As I was preparing it for entry, I looked up at the narrow staircase and saw a rather large black snake, head standing straight up, sitting on one of the steps. As it turned out, it was not harmful, just one of those creatures which look for food in unoccupied buildings and actually do a good job of eliminating mice. However, it looked more like a very dangerous rattle snake to me and I raced to my car phone to get my dependable handyman out to the house to get rid of it. Unlike me, he was a big Swedish guy afraid of nothing! Something that day about the snake gave me the shivers like an 'ominous' warning about the house but I shook off the feeling. After all, this deal was too good to be true. I had negotiated the rent down to $275 a month with an option to buy and my lover had agreed to get back together and live in the house with me. Why was I still feeling that there was some unknown force driving me? Since my gall bladder operation three years earlier, life just wasn't the same anymore. I was the same person and yet, I was someone I didn't know at all. It was as if a VEIL had been drawn over me. I could see clearly through it, but my world around me was ever changing and unpredictable. Although sometimes I was uncomfortable with the changes, I just attributed it all to the new and exciting challenges of life which I had created and then found myself in. After all, I was a self made millionaire. I alone controlled everything in my life, that was for sure…(at least, I thought that was for sure!). Gordon, my general all around handyman arrived quickly, cut the lawn down to size with heavy city owned equipment, removed the large black snake then went and picked up all of my furniture as well as Judy's and arrived at our new residence. He was a big boned Swedish guy who could wrap his giant arms around just about anything of major weight, pick it up and carry it all by himself. He was his own stage show and something which you had to see to believe.

Playing House

Chapter 4

PLAYING HOUSE

(Judy)

Oh, the excitement of moving! I hadn't been this happy in a long time. To move in a beautiful huge home in a prominent country area of town with the man I adore. What more can I ask for? We picked up all the children and brought them to the house. They actually all fit together like a set of gears at the ages of 6, 7, 8 and 9. I was very excited for my children but I wanted his boys to also feel the excitement and let them know right away that they would be with us every weekend, every holiday and a lot of weeks during the summer. I was starting a beautiful new life. All my troubles were over, or so I thought! The joy of 'newness'....it's so exciting, why can't it remain?

"Stan, Joyce is on the phone". Every time she called, the anger and jealousy arose in me. I had divorced Joe the previous year and Stan is still legally married! What the heck is this all about? We're living together and he's still married? I felt like a kept woman. Am I being deceived? It was all so beautiful for a while but then the quarrels and fighting began. Every time we had a fight, I got in my newest purchase, a yellow Fiat spider convertible and went out for a fast spin to nowhere. I became another person outside of that house. I loved Stan and his boys but it was certainly a different life style than I was used to. Our new home was always filled with activities. Friends and acquaintances loved hanging out there. It was a house filled with fun and parties; FOR NOW! My friend Myra had to move to a smaller house and we decided to let her oldest daughter Desi move in with us. Myra had three girls by three different husbands. Desi was not the most liked of the three and needed a family to really love on her so we took her in as one of our own. She was almost 15 and we thought it would also be good to have a permanent sitter on the premises as we were out a lot. "Desi, watch the kids for a while Stan and I have to go into town. Keep a sharp eye on them, Ok.?" It was one of those times when Steven and Elliot were visiting. On returning home, all of the kids ran out to the car to tattle on whatever each of them was into. "Mom", Holly cried, "Steven and Kurt almost burned the house down!" "What?... where are the boys now?" I could feel my heart beat faster as I thought about what might have happened. "Kurt! Stevie! What did you do?" The boys started to answer all at once. "We wanted to light a campfire like our cub scout pack does" "IN THE HOUSE!" I yelled! "Yeah mom, downstairs in the old dirt cellar but don't worry about it Steven sat on it and it went out!" Stan's normal happy face turned very serious as he jumped into the confusion.

(Stan)

"Judy, let me handle this. Ok. boys, get your coats on, we're taking a trip down to the fire department. "Stan", I cut in, "its kind of late in the evening don't you think?" "Judy! I said, let ME handle this! Look, Karen's husband is a fireman; we know all of them at the fire house. These boys need a real fast lesson in what they did". The boys returned an hour later after seeing a film on what fires can really do. Their faces were pale as they came into the house. "O.K. guys, Stan said in a very stern voice. I got you each ten books of matches. You're going to sit out on the front steps and light one match at a time and if I see you lighting more than one at a time, you'll just have to start all over again. I don't think you will be too excited to ever try lighting a fire again here, right?"

"You know somethin' Jude, I don't know about Kurt, but I've never seen Stevie act like this before. What d'ya think would ever have driven them to do such a dumb thing?"

(Judy)

"**Desi!**" I yelled, as soon as Stan pulled out of the driveway with the boys. "Where were you when they were lighting fires in the cellar?" "HUH" she answered with a typical teenage dumb look on her face, "Hey Jude, the last time I saw them they were in their bedroom and I went back into my room. They must have snuck downstairs after that. I dunno, hey look, the house didn't burn down did it?" "Didn't you hear all the commotion going on at all?" I asked, more and more aggravated with her with every question. "Guess not" she answered; obviously the only thing she wanted was to go back to her comfortable bed. I knew that Stan would take care of the situation but I was more concerned about their heads and what they were thinking plus, they were all fearful of the dark dingy basement or.....was it more my fears?

I loved walking around the property. There were so many beautiful trees and flowers in full bloom. I also loved our two neighbor guys who lived in the back house. I always heard their dog barking so one day I went to the back of their house to see Shabam. She was a Dobie Shepherd. They named her after gunfire and were trying to raise her up to be a hunting dog. The guys weren't home and there she was ensnared in the bushes with her leash wrapped around her in the hot sun so I decided to untie her and bring her into our house for a while. I fell in love with this puppy dog and kept on loving her as much as I could be around her. Wrong move! I didn't realize I wasn't supposed to do that because she was being trained to hunt, not to be passive. The kids loved on her a lot too. She would run after them whenever she got free from her leash. The guys in the back weren't very happy with me though, as I was breaking the training she was getting but my thoughts were always that she was a better lover for a family than she would be as a killer in the wild.

"OH NO". My heart sunk a little as I saw Cliff looking for Shabam one day. "Hi Cliff", I managed to say as innocently as I could. "I rescued Shabam a week ago when she got tangled up in your bushes. She looked so thirsty and the sun was so hot" "Hey Judy look, I decided for all good purposes, Shabam is really not any use to me and my roommate anymore. She breaks free and always wants to run over here to be with you and the kids so we're giving you the dog". "Yea, thanks Cliff I never meant to have that happen but we'll love her and take good care of her" I could have said all kinds of nice things but I could tell by his voice that he really wasn't very happy about the situation. Shabam had to be house trained as well now and when bed time came around she whined and barked a lot. It wasn't as easy as I thought. There was even a time when we all thought about giving her back but thank goodness we didn't. We also had to break her of her habit of wandering off the property and killing some neighbor's chickens. I knew a lot of my friends in the police department, so did Stan and they were always being called to pick up Shabam at one house or another in our area. The police would always bring her back with a huge warning to us. Thank goodness Stan broke her of that habit especially after she ate our rabbit. Our son Kurt went outside and saw all the rabbit hairs and began to cry and started to hit Shabam and yelled at her to "spit it out", as if she really could! Although there was some 'sick' humor in the whole thing, we were all really upset with that scene and had to work really hard with the dog, but she turned out to be a trusted member of the family.

Whenever we returned to the house after shopping or whatever, the children ran all at once to the car to greet us. "Stan! Here they come, wonder what happened while we were away this time?" We usually looked at each other and said "goodbye" 'cause we wouldn't be able to talk to each other for a long time. "Stan, Dad, Judy, Mom, they all yelled with Desi standing right behind them. These guys came to the door and they had big guns and said they were looking for a guy named Joel. They weren't very nice and demanded to know who we were" "Desi", I said feeling some fear getting to me, "what did you tell them?" "Hey, I just told them we were renting this house and we didn't have any idea who this Joel person was. We were all so scared Judy, we were afraid they wouldn't believe us but they did. They also said that they would be back though!" "Ok. Des, sorry we weren't here for you all but we'll find out who this Joel guy is...sounds like part of the mafia or something". The state we were living in had a reputation of being really involved in mafia business so it was no surprise when I remembered a time when Joe and I wanted to buy a vending machine and the mafia approached us and demanded a portion of the proceeds. Of course, they always said that was for our 'protection', whatever that meant. Protection from who? Them? Right! We do the investment; we do the work and give them half the profit! We sent the machines back to the company. That was my first taste of how the mafia works with their businesses.

"Listen everyone", I said firmly," do not open the door for anyone you don't know....do you hear me? In the future we'll call the house and check up on all of you...Ok.?" Inside I was hoping those thugs at the door wouldn't come back, but I was wrong.

(Stan)

"Hey Jude, I met Cliff in the back house again and he told me that there really was a guy named Joel who lived in this house before and that as far as he knew he was connected with the mafia and that there was a murder of the gal who lived with him. Something to do with a lot of money he stole from them too! Cliff said that he heard later that Joel moved all the furniture out of the house overnight and that he might have moved to Florida. Boy, I bet this house has a lot of history linked to it over the years, huh? HEY! who are those guys now walking all over the property? WHOA, one of them is knocking at the front door!" "**You Joel?**" the guy at the door demanded in a loud threatening voice. I noticed a revolver hanging in a shoulder strap just beneath his jacket. Other guys on the property looked real ugly too but it didn't take me ten seconds to respond just as firmly. I grew up in this mafia controlled state and I could play the game just as good as them. **"NO"**, I responded, "as far as I was told he moved to Florida. He used to own this house but I rent it now, just me and my family. Get off the property now or I'll have the police here in seconds!" Sha-Bam was by my side. If she suspected you were friendly, even if you were a complete stranger, she'd lead you right to the silverware and valuables and lick your face while doing it. But, if she suspected danger, she could growl and flash her teeth at you just as quick! The guy at the door backed away at my reaction to him as well as looking at the dog and left the property in a hurry with his goons.

"God, Jude, can you believe that? Guess there's some real truth to what Cliff told me huh?" "Stan that makes me real nervous you know, I mean....with the kids here and everything. All of a sudden I don't feel as safe here" Judy talked with some obvious fear as she processed what had just happened and I couldn't blame her for being concerned, especially about the kids' safety, as well as our own. "Look hon, those guys won't return, they'll check out who we are through the bank. Ya know what I told you, the bank that owns this house is mafia controlled. Most of its money is from gamblin' and drugs and stuff. Hey, unless someone has a jail record, they can't even get elected to run the government in this state. Check it out! I grew up right around the corner from one of the biggest hoods in the entire New England area and I was even in the National Guard with one of his sons. Some of the stories he would tell us was really bad news. "O.K. Stan" Judy said, in a half believing tone, I'll relax about it, but I still don't like the idea that gangster types are prowling all over here looking for this Joel guy". Judy calmed down, and I hoped what I said would sooth her nerves but I had to admit, although I sounded real tough at the front door, inside me I was also shaken up a bit by the encounter. Our little storybook dwelling had suddenly acquired an uncomfortable 'spirit' associated with it. But, as days went on, the incident was talked about more with humor than with fear. As far as the children were concerned, they were never confronted with the incident again. But, our curiosity about the supposed murder of whoever the gal was that lived here with Joel grew to us questioning Cliff and anyone else who might know more about the details. We even searched every nook and cranny of the house and barn to see what we could discover. The dirt cellar of the house was old and musty and during the daytime it felt O.K. to rummage around in it. It was mostly empty except for the furnace and my large safe which I had Gordon move there, and it had a small eerie looking darkened crawl space under the sunroom area which was probably an add on over the years. At night however, there were times I would go down to check on the furnace and as I climbed back up the stairs quickly, I felt a shiver running up my back as if there was someone right behind me. The kids also reported the same feeling once in a while, especially our daughter Holly. As a result, no one ever went down there at night. If it was necessary, it was usually me that went. It only had two small light bulbs hanging from two antique type shaded fixtures which only added to the creepy feeling of being down ther

Time flew by and my mini real estate empire was dissolving before my very eyes. Mortgage payments fell way behind, accelerated loan payments, tenant problems and property expenses drained my accounts to dangerously low levels. I convinced myself that I would be better off without all the headaches involved with all of it so I declared bankruptcy and let all the properties be auctioned off including the house that my ex wife and boys lived in. They could move in with her mother nearby and, after all, if I did that and, sold off certain assets, including my sharp white T-Bird, I'd still have enough money left to live comfortably in my new home with my beautiful Judy and find a new business venture to start and include her in it as well. I stood on the sidewalk one sunny morning as I witnessed some of my holdings being sold off to some investors. To my amazement, as well as my attorney's, I felt no sorrow whatsoever. As a matter of fact, I was greatly relieved and delivered from all of the pressures associated with it. I had also dissolved my 'potna-ship" the month before with Dennis, who by then I considered to be the brother I never had, and I managed to rent out all of our real estate and construction offices to a couple who ran a women's clothing store by the name of "**Just Things**". The name Just Things was ironic when I thought of the first words I ever said to Denny about Judy when he said she had a 'thing' for me and I had replied..."Yeah...and I have a 'thing' for her!" It all seemed so surreal. Everything in me was screaming to save it all but I could do nothing more than laugh about it. I even heard a voice inside me repeating the words *"you'll never recover from the loss"*. The tone of that internal voice was more threatening than factual but I shrugged those impressions off quickly. After all, I had made it all once, I'll do it again. Three months before selling the T-Bird, I noticed that the front license plate was missing and then the rear plate as well. It was a very disturbing 'omen' in that the plates were Vanity plates with my three initials. I reported them stolen and was given 'funky' average plates waiting for my vanity replacements when Cal, the sidewalk cop stopped me one day and told me he had seen my plates on another car somewhere. I was never able to regain my prize vanity plates again.

I had also managed to rent out one of the on street storefronts, which I had previously owned, to myself but had put the lease in

Judy's name before the bankruptcy proceedings began. Over the last few months, junk jewelry had become the hottest new fashion item on the market nationally. Since I had worked in the industry previously and since we were located in a state loaded with jewelry manufacturers, it seemed like the perfect solution to start a new venture. My Irish friend Smitty came up with the name of **"Pointless Forest"** for the jewelry store operation during a party time while smoking pot. "Pointless Forest was a fable by Harry Nillson which stated;

"I was on acid and I looked at the trees and I realized that they all came to points, and the little branches came to points, and the houses came to points. I thought, 'Oh! Everything has a point, and if it doesn't, then there's no point to it.'"

Since there seemed to be 'no point' to anything I was doing then, it made excellent sense and '*a point*' to name the store by that name. (The veil over my mind seemed to have gotten a lot cloudier, but the excitement of a totally new beginning pushed aside all practical business sense).

"Hey Jude", I said loudly as we sat having a small glass of wine in our new country kitchen. "How'd ja like to travel to New York City every month and other big cities and get involved with jewelry accessory trade shows?" "What?" she answered with a huge smile. Her beautiful big green eyes got even bigger as she contemplated the thought and the excitement of the sound of jewelry and the additional idea of traveling. "I'd love it Stan, but what do you mean, I don't understand how we're going to do that". "Look Jude, you know the empty storefront in one of my former buildings that I owned…..well I rented it to myself but I put the lease in your name for a ridiculously low monthly rent. It already has some built in counters in it. Couldn't do it in my name 'cause of my impending bankruptcy but the lease has a lot of exit clauses in it anyway, so if it doesn't work out, we'll just close the place down and walk out. Your credit won't be hurt one bit. Whad'ya think hon?" "WOW, sounds great Stan when do we start". "Crab eyes, I've already bought a bunch of sample lines at wholesale and you can go with me soon to pick out more of what you like. We don't have to pay much of anything for the exterior signage, I can do that at home myself and we can, ya know, decorate it all inside real cheap…I know you'd love having fun doing that. Like the idea?"

In addition to Jude, 'Crab eyes' was just one of the many pet names I called my new soul mate. 'Buns' was another after her firmly shaped backside. 'Little head' after her small but nicely shaped head and "Freckles" still another. (Her body had many and I loved every one of them). 'Judith' was her real birth name and one of the names that I always held for last and the name I always said as a question when I wanted to know an immediate answer. When I dragged it out, it was always in a more demanding voice but she never took it negatively.

(Judy)

"I love this house Stan but there are times I get a funny feeling that someone is always behind me". Stan didn't say a word but I felt that he had the same feelings but was afraid to voice them.

Time went on and we had a lot of fun as a family especially when Stan's boys came to visit for the weekend. I loved having them here and wished they could live here all the time but every time he went to pick them up I felt resentment building inside me. Still no divorce with Stan and his wife. He was waiting for her to file first. Every time he would pick up the boys I would ask him if he had spoken to her and the arguments and fights would begin. I was beginning to be a tyrant when it came to this subject. Stan had a very deep and loud voice and when he yelled he wouldn't drop the matter and went on and on. I noticed that I was starting to pick up some habits from my childhood and began to hide in the closet under the clothes until he stopped. It was a reminder of my mom, whom I was so fearful of when she yelled at me. It represented such a strong authority and I had no strength in me to come against authoritative people. Finally, he stopped his yelling but I stayed hidden for a while. "Maybe he'll worry about my whereabouts", I thought silently. I didn't like what I was becoming and what was happening to us. I only wanted to experience the love we had when we first met but I wondered more and more if that ever lasts. As I crawled out of the closet, I stayed in the bedroom until Stan came in. He made many good points about his wife divorcing him first because it would make her feel better. She had done very little wrong in their marriage; he had just fallen out of love. I knew that Stan was a very compassionate man but my jealously and insecurity was overtaking me. Finally, the day came when the divorce papers were delivered. It took forever but now his wife could move on and we were free. I didn't know why it was so important for me, except for my insecurities. I just knew that I didn't want any part of marriage in my life again for a very long time.

(Stan)

Our new jewelry store "Pointless Forest" was not a smashing success, but it was holding its own somehow and with the Christmas holiday season approaching, we were looking for local or statewide gift shows to be a part of. The door swung open and a guy walked in somewhat clumsily with leather handbags hanging off both arms. "You the owners?" he asked very loudly. "My name's Ken. My wife Linda and I own a Turquoise store in the next town and I import leather goods from Mexico as well. I have a lot of bags in stock. I'm just traveling around to see if anyone wants to buy some or even take them on consignment. Your store looks like it could use some hard to find accessories to display". "What do you think Jude?", I asked, unsure of taking on a totally different product line. "Boy Stan, I really like these handbags, they look really well made, and I haven't seen anything like them anywhere else". The more we talked, the more we liked Ken's cheerful spirit and his aggressive salesmanship. "Ok Ken, why don't you leave us with a small assortment of your bags and we'll see how they sell". "Look you guys", he responded "whatever you get for them I'll split half the profit, Ok? And by the way, I'm going to be in a craft show soon, maybe you should be a part of it, you might do pretty good with your jewelry too". I looked at the printed brochure about the show. "Hey look Judy; this is the same craft show that Smitty told us about. Yeah Ken, we'll be there, we know about it already from a friend of ours. Hey, let's get together sometime before the show. Tell you what, Jude and I will come out to your store soon O.K.? Maybe we can get together with your wife sometime too". "Sounds like a plan to me, see yas soon, just give me a call when you want to come by. I'm all alone and my hours are crazy" he answered as he walked out the door. "Oy Vey", I thought, Another Irishman in my life but I knew I would like Ken the minute he walked in the store. He had the same 'cocky' attitude that Smitty had. I just hoped he was a little more stable, but then Judy and I loved being around fun people who knew how to enjoy life.

Since I had sold my beautiful white T-Bird, we bought Desi's mom's Olds Toranado that she had for sale before moving. It was large, black and comfortable but a lot less impressive than anything I was used to driving. It even had headlights with shades that lifted up when the lights were on and shut when off. But one of them didn't work too good and flipped up and down as I drove, kind-a looked like the car was winking at everyone. It was a far cry from my personal taste and I felt like a jerk driving it but, it was affordable and comfortable and served the purpose for now.

Judy and I made a few trips to wholesale jewelry outlets in the state including a trip to New York City as well. During one of those trips, we decided to have Bobby, a young guy that Judy had counseled at the Youth Center in town, stay in our house and help Desi watch the kids while we were away. When we returned, the same welcoming committee ran out to the car. "We were robbed", they all yelled at once. The sight of four children, an overweight teenager, a dog jumping and squealing, (she didn't really have a bark) and a newcomer surrounding us was very overwhelming to say the least. "WHAT!" we answered in shock. "What happened?" "Stan, Judy", Bobby said in a convincing tone. "We all went for a long walk and when we returned, there were things turned over and stuff all over the floor. I don't know what was robbed but something must have been, you better look around". Soon after Judy went upstairs to our bedroom, I heard her scream, "STAN, my diamond ring and camera are missing and some money I had stashed away for the kids is gone". We also had allowed Bobby to hold down the fort at the store sometimes and even do some cash register sales. It always seemed like there was some cash missing but not enough to connect any of it to Bobby. It was getting to the point that we were getting very hesitant to leave the kids alone with anyone anymore and it was definitely getting in the way of our desire to move around and travel. Our freedom was being controlled and we didn't like the whole idea of it, but we were also very responsible parents so we kept finding ourselves more in more of a dilemma as to how to solve the problem. It seemed that our whole relationship was changing and causing a lot of stress we hadn't counted on.

Decisions which I had always been able to make clearly and effectively in the past seemed to backfire a lot. "***Was I listening to another 'voice'*** inside me or what" I thought. Life had been so simple with my former wife. Why was it getting so complicated, I wondered. After all, I had always loved 'newness', challenges and new experiences but since Judy and I met, our lives had been turned topsie turvie. We found out later that Bobby had been threatened by his older brother who was on drugs, to rob our house and he was also taking small amounts of cash from the store as well. Besides, he was the only other person who knew where the kid's money was hidden. Bobby had even scattered some loose change over the floor to make the scene look real and had found a whole bag of marijuana that I had hidden as well. My reaction was very violent. I even went to his house and threatened him in front of his mother if he and his older brother didn't return everything but I couldn't prove it so that never happened. We learned a hard lesson and as a result our search for more responsible folks to watch over our family began.

(Judy)

"Judy, I have to run some errands, can you handle the store alone?" "HELLO! Stan? They're not exactly banging the door down to get in. You go, I've got it covered". "Ok. Jude, I may come back or just meet you at home." Love ya babe, drive careful". Although it always felt good to be totally in charge, it was too quiet so I decided to crank up the music. Just then I looked up and saw a young couple coming in carrying a couple of jewelry cases. "HI", I said excitedly, seeing new faces and activity around me. "Welcome to Pointless Forest, I'm Judy and you are?" "I'm Charles and this is my wife Sara. Hmmm, Pointless Forest, I gotta say that's an interesting name for a store". "Well, yeah it's interesting all right a friend of ours named it for us, what can I do for you?" "If you have a few minutes, Sara and I would like to show you some handcrafted jewelry made in Mexico". "Sure" I replied, "boy these are beautiful, what do you call the stones. or are they shells?" "They're called Abalone shells and they're set in sterling silver. We have our own import business and travel to interior Mexico to a town called Taxco way up in the mountains to purchase it. Taxco has one of the largest silver mines in the world". After viewing all of their samples I felt the jewelry would be a great item for the store, it would certainly class up the merchandise. "I can't make any decisions though without discussing it with my partner and letting him see it all, can we set up an appointment for tomorrow morning?" "Sorry, Sara and I are just passing through, won't be here overnight". "Oh no, I really want him to see it too. Let me call him at home and see if we can get together today, do you have some time?" "All right we do but how 'bout we go get some lunch and come back later?" "Great, that'll give me some time to get my partner to come here by the time you get back. Have a great lunch, see you later". I was so excited, I loved the jewelry. I called Stan but he wasn't at home. Darn, no answer. Half an hour later Stan decided to stop by the store before going home. "STAN! Your timing is awesome, I'm so excited. You have to meet these people who are coming back here soon. They're selling some really beautiful jewelry, it's all made in Mexico, you gotta see it!" "**Judy! Judy!** Calm down, what people? What jewelry?" I started to explain it to Stan and just then Charles and Sara walked in.

After a brief introduction they showed Stan the line of abalone and sterling. "Wow! these are really nice and different than anything I've seen anywhere", he said with the same excitement I had over it. "Stan, let's buy some of it, it'll brighten up the line of jewelry we have and we can take it to the Craft Show that's coming up soon". After picking out all the pieces we wanted we waited quietly to find out the cost of all of it. **$900 bucks!** Wow, we both bit our lips a little. "Really Stan, if we're going to get into this business big time, we have to buy more than $2 items". "O.K. hon, you're right!" After the couple left, we both choked a little about the money we just spent but we knew it was the right move. I was really happy that they also had a catalog to leave us so we could buy more. Little did we knew that from a $900 purchase a whole new business would begin. It seemed that we were getting into products from Mexico, purses from Ken and Lin and abalone shell jewelry from Charles and Sara. I was so excited all the time. I never had any kind of business before. It was all new to me and I really liked both couples. Soon after our meeting with Charles and Sara, we went to Ken & Lin's store in the next town. "Wow Ken, you have some awesome leather goods here and your turquoise jewelry is gorgeous! Where do you get it all from?" "Hey, only the best, Kingman mines in Arizona and all the leather goods from Mexico, you know, you have some of the bags!" "Hey Ken, wait 'till you see the abalone and sterling silver jewelry we just bought we'll have all of our stuff at the craft show, should be fun huh?'

Days rolled by and the few customers that came in went straight for the Mexican jewelry we just bought. As our sales increased I thought to myself, "you have to invest to be prosperous", way out of my league but I was learning. Stan returned to take over the store and I was on my way home to see my children. Store hours were getting on our nerves somewhat. The kids were home all day with Desi and school wasn't starting again for another couple of weeks. As I drove around to the back of the house, Desi, Kurt and Holly ran out to the car to greet me. "JUDE!" Desi blurted all at once, "Holly was riding her bike outside and a couple in a car drove half way up the driveway and a woman opened the door and I saw them from the window and I didn't have a good feeling about it and the lady got out and then I saw Shabam growling and running across the lawn towards them and then the lady jumped back in the car and they drove off real fast!" "O.K., slow down tell me what happened Holly. "Mommy, you always taught me to be careful with strangers so when she asked me if I lived here I told her no, I was just visiting my friend. The lady and the man in the car wanted me to get in the car because their little boy wanted a friend to play with and then they would bring me home later. They even wanted to give me some candy but I said no to them again and then Shabam came running towards us growling and the lady jumped back in the car and they backed out real fast and drove away!"

I loved this property, but there was always some funny stuff going on that gave me the jitters sometimes. I didn't want to show the panic I was feeling to Holly so I just tried to keep calm and went in the house to call the Police. Holly was a pretty sharp little girl for a seven year old. She even remembered two of the numbers on the license plate and Desi described the car. When the Officer arrived, he questioned Holly and she told him everything she told me. The Officer knew, like I did, that Holly was almost abducted but I could tell that he really didn't want to push the issue 'cause there were no other reports in the area. The following day at the store, I was still nervously recovering from the thought of my little girl almost being kidnapped when Cal, the town traffic cop come in. I thought he had some news about the incident but he was only there to collect some overdue parking tickets I had. The town was small and I knew Cal real well from the Youth Center I worked at. "Ok. Cal", I said real bluntly, "before we get to the tickets I owe what's the Police Department doing about the incident with my Daughter yesterday?" "What do you mean Judy? What incident?" he answered, completely ignorant of the situation. "You don't know? Your buddy Frank was out to my house and filed a report about it!". "Judy, I was on duty last night. I never saw any report like that". "WHAT? Hey, this isn't your everyday traffic ticket Cal....this is about a couple that nearly abducted my daughter!". "Look Judy, I'll check into it Ok.?" "By the way Cal, you know what you can do with these traffic tickets, I won't pay one dime until this matter is investigated". Two whole weeks went by and nothing more was done, not until a little boy down the road was actually abducted and not found.

"Stan, we are so lucky I feel so bad for that little boy's family, it could have been Holly! I'm so thankful that she remembered what I taught her and thank goodness for Shabam scaring them off. It's amazing that she's such a passive dog but when she feels danger she's right there. Things like this happen everywhere but never to people like us right?" It took a long time to get over the uneasy feelings I kept having over the whole thing.

Stan and I realized shortly after that running a retail store wasn't for us and there really weren't enough customers to keep it open anyway so we decided within a few months to close it. The craft show had opened by then and it was a complete success. We brought our three parakeets and bamboo cage there to give the booth some added interest. People would stop to see the birds and then the jewelry. Oh what fun we had. Stan and I had never done anything like this before. It was a completely new adventure for us. Every night as we brought the birds home, we had to cover up the birdcage so they wouldn't get chilled from the freezing cold weather outside and then, bring them back the next day. Our close friends Denny and Jackie visited us at the show, and we met some new friends Doug and Gale who sold homemade fudge...."fudge people", that was a good name for them, they were so friendly and he was such a comedian. After a few weeks the show ended and we all went home and celebrated. By this time it was Stan's holiday of Chanukah and my Christmas holiday at the same time. Strangely enough, this was the only thing we didn't have in common. Although it bothered us sometimes, we just referred to it as "My God and Your God". That was also strange because we really only celebrated the traditions. He had been Bar Mitzvahed and I had been baptized when we were both in our early teens but we had no real understanding about God in any true sense. Stan was raised as a Conservative Jew and he considered me to be a 'Heinz57 variety Christian'. I had been brought up in a bunch of different churches and married Joe who was a Catholic. So, it was all the same mumbo jumbo to me. But Stan and I always had a lot of fun celebrating both holidays together since we met, especially with our ecumenical house full of children. Walking in the woods on our property that summer, we picked out the tree we would cut down for Christmas and then bring the kids with us and drag it through the snow. The smell of fresh cut pine filled the house.

Stan called it his Chanukah bush. He was very creative and usually was the one who did most of the decorations on it as well. We lit a fire, had hot chocolate and really enjoyed the holiday time together as a family. It was a perfect end to a hectic year. (or so we thought**!**) In our search for some Christmas gifts for some friends, we came across a little store in town called The Flaming

Cauldron. Although we talked to the owner about our jewelry line, we were more fascinated with all sorts of strange items in the store. It even had a back room full of what we discovered to be Trolls made in Tennessee. There were lots of them, all sizes and shapes. All were made out of wood with funny hair on top, and most of them had red eyes. The female trolls were smooth wood and the male trolls were rough with big hairy mustaches. We decided to buy one with white hair for our house because the lady that ran the place said it would bring good luck. It was very rare and also the only 'Albino' troll she had left. She was dressed in dark purple and with her strange jewelry and weird hat; she definitely fit the look and feeling of the shop she was running. "Hey Jude, look at this" Stan said with amazement. On our way out he noticed a whole rack of witchcraft potion starter sets and wanted to buy one. I was curious but grabbed him and left quickly because I started to get real funny 'vibes' about the whole place. I felt a lot of darkness like a VEIL, trying to creep all over us. It was the end of 1975 and the beginning of everything good and great, or so I thought! I never had a good feeling about that Troll from the minute I laid eyes on it!

Albino Troll

DECEIVING SPIRITS

"Hey babe", Stan mumbled, "winter is really here huh?" I was thinking, now that our store is shut we may as well just travel around and sell our inventory at wholesale....you know...a lot of stores have to replenish some of their stock after the holidays. Could be fun and profitable and we'd be traveling around a lot. No sense hangin' around an empty house all day with the kids in school ya know? "Hmmm, O.K. luvie, what do we do first" "Well we'll just stop wherever we find a store that looks interesting and give it a shot....how 'bout it". "I'm with you hon" I replied with new sense of adventure. Days turned into weeks and in between our sales trips, we found ourselves getting together more and more with Ken and Lin, the turquoise jewelry people as well as Stan's former 'pot-na' Denny and his girlfriend Jackie, the tall redhead he had met at the Harborside Tavern. Our schedule got pretty busy with Ken and Lin who loved to go with us to different clubs during the week where Disco dance music was the rage. They had their mothers to baby sit their two boys and we had Desi at our house all the time. We all had 'Dance Fever" like the song title said..."staying alive". Ken and Stan both loved to smoke weed but Lin and I not as much. Sometimes we would also sneak a small bottle of wine in one of our large purses and just keep filling up the four glasses under the table that we had ordered in order to save money. The weeks turned into months, and before we knew it spring had come and gone and summer was upon us. Dance fever had never been more fun, especially with our new friends Ken and Lin. Den and Jackie, on the other hand, were more the home-body type so they were reserved for the week end get together. Occasionally, we made plans for an overnight trip somewhere for kicks. Stan and Jackie always hit it off comically with a lot of joking about silly things. I was a lot quieter especially when all three of them were smoking pot. I never really enjoyed it but found myself getting high just being around all the exhaled smoke, especially in the car. Stan was always the driver with me next to him and them in the back seat. One time he was convinced that the car wouldn't make it up the hill and couldn't figure out how to turn it around. Another time on a highway, he announced to all of us... "I don't know how to tell you guys this but I see hands on the wheel and they're not mine!" Jackie would lean over and slap Stan on the head and say... "Get this car in control you fool". We'd all laugh a lot and were lucky that there were hardly any other cars around us. Stan and Denny still loved to party and even though I knew better I found myself being drawn into strange new situations that were too much fun not to be a part of. Returning home by ourselves once during a dark midnight hour from a full day on the beach, our suits were still a little damp. We hadn't changed to dry clothes and since we were completely alone on back roads in total darkness we took the wet suits off while driving and hung them on the outside mirrors to dry. We had forgotten that we still had to drive over a really big bridge with a toll booth at the end and had no time to stop. Well, there we were, "in the raw" as we pulled up to the brightly lit toll booth and its lone male attendant inside, no other cars in sight. Stan searched frantically for two dollars in his pants that were crumpled up on the floor. We both smiled nervously and could hardly hold ourselves from laughing out loud as Stan handed him a $5 bill which had to be changed by the attendant. The attendant's eyes got so big; I thought they would pop right out of his head! We laughed all the way home and upon getting there we barely managed to get inside the house before attacking each other passionately in a dark area of the lawn.

Alone in the house one day I looked around and saw that strange looking troll Stan had bought just sitting there staring at me with its white hairy body and big red eyes. Those eyes seemed to follow me wherever I went. The store owner at The Flaming Cauldron said it was very good luck to own. A lady she knew had bought one, placed it in her window and one day her house had caught fire and burned down. No one was hurt and the only possession left was the troll. The troll, she said, had protected the lady from harm. I never really had ever given that statement any thought but what a bunch of bunk and "deception" that was! She lost everything in the fire but the Troll survived! I brushed aside the feelings, after all Stan had bought it only as a gift for me and a thing to joke about. I loved to dance and blasted the music. I was all alone except for the troll. Sometimes it felt good to be alone in the house but somehow even then I always felt something around me. Looking around my home as I danced, I felt so happy; it was so pretty and big with its double fireplace and large sunroom with all the hanging plants. Stan and I had rented a small office not far from town but it got too expensive so we moved all the jewelry into the sunroom. Everything was stored in bins and every piece was priced and numbered. Stan had hand drawn each item, priced it and created a catalog. Our friend Smitty, the Irish "leprechaun" had helped us, once again, to name our newest company **SAJA Imports**. SA after Stan's initials and JA after mine. The catalog was a brilliant decision as we were now able to send it to a lot of our customers so they could place orders without us having to travel state to state. We had fun with the business and even had the children help pack some of it to be shipped. We also gave each of them a pencil and paper and asked them to design pieces of jewelry that maybe we could have made in Mexico. They really surprised us with some of their creative ideas.

(Stan)

"Boy Jude, the kids really came up with some good designs, I mean they're simple but I could include some of them somehow. I'll put it together and we'll call Charles up and get him to order us some samples from Taxco. You know, we oughta fly down there ourselves this year and eliminate the 'middle' man". "But Stan, is that the right thing to do? I mean, after all, we should tell Charles and Sara first don't you think?" "Naah! Look Jude, business is business, can't worry about being honest all the time, ya gotta do what's profitable". "Well I still think we should tell them but you're the boss…hey, I'd love to travel to Mexico, when do you think"? (The plan still bothered my basic nature of being honest, but I couldn't seem to argue against what I felt was wrong). "Hon, I'll check the airfares, and we'll need to get an adult in here to watch the kids and Desi too and plan a date. She's good but I wouldn't trust her for a whole week with that responsibility. **Hey babe**, ya know what?" "What now Stan?" (Stan was always coming up with new ideas…sometimes I couldn't keep up with it, much less go along with it). "Well, we've been in the house for a long time, working hard and I think it's time to throw a big house party. The kids are with Joe this weekend and my boys are going somewhere with their mom, we have the whole weekend to ourselves. Let's invite all our friends and their friends..and..how 'bout the new owner of the property in the back house? Now that Cliffy has moved out and Arnie is there with his girlfriend Janet he'd be insulted if we didn't have them over too and anyway, he always has some really good pot to smoke. We'll start it on Friday at whatever and let it go 'till it ends…what d'ya think? Good booze, good weed, loud music who's gonna hear us? We're on four acres…who cares anyway? Let's PAAARTY!!!" "O.K. lovies, I'll do the invites, you get the booze. But Stan, you know, we like people for who they are but some of them don't really like each other. You think that could be a problem?" "HEY Jude, that's their problem, not ours. They'll find people to have fun with; I bet we'll get a couple of dozen people or more to come here".

(Judy)

Stan was right, lots of people came on and off, like 40 or more and the party went on for two whole days. Sometimes we went upstairs to take a short nap and when we would return, there were new people in the house. One guy who was invited by a casual friend of ours turned up and stayed the whole night. Neither Stan nor I had a prejudiced bone in our body but this was a black guy and everyone else was white. He really had a sense of humor when we questioned who he was. He looked at us with a big smile and just said "Wow, I didn't think you noticed!" After we got downstairs the second morning, he was washing some dishes and glasses for us. I was beginning to feel like we were a couple leading a double life. Sometimes we were the upright concerned parents and sometimes the "who cares party people". There was even a small pond nearby that some people went swimming in the nude. We went there a few times, but there were also a few younger guys that I had counseled at the now closed Youth Center in town and I felt really uncomfortable with them staring at us, so that ended that.

But, something was really exciting about it all and I found myself dreaming of sexual fantasies a lot. Stan was of course a willing partner so the same passion that drove us together in the beginning just kept on increasing as time went on. I sure wasn't the same person I'd always known. Was I deceiving myself about that or was I being deceived? Sometimes I felt so confused about who I was becoming!

"Hey did you know your insurance guy Garry and his new girlfriend have a Sheepdog puppy for sale? I asked him about it at the party. The dog has title papers a mile long, he's a real valuable dog but they can't keep him. I've always wanted a big sheepdog, you know, like in the movie *Please Don't Eat the Daisies*. He'd look great sitting next to me in my little yellow spider convertible...and Stan...he's only $100!" "You're kidding Jude...right...another dog here? We got Shabam; we got two cats Holly brought in. Remember how she made the school bus stop so she could get out and pick up the stray cat? Then there are the two parakeets. We still could have had three, but remember the night Desi's mother came in at one o'clock in the morning 'cause she needed to see you about a problem she had and the bird flew 'round 'n round in the cage and dropped dead just as she came in the front door and how Desi's mom screamed... "I killed your bird" We didn't know whether to cry or laugh! "Oh yeah, how 'bout the rabbit that died of frostbite outside and the one we still have and the giant Tortoise 'Stella" I bought for Stevie and Elliot? What the hell, sure, what's another animal or two? How 'bout naming him Rufus...you know...after the rock group? RUFUS?"..."yeah Stan...I like that name. Let's go look at him".

When we got to the insurance guy's girlfriend's house, we saw a box full of little puppies and what looked like the mother dog sitting there. Wrong, it was Rufus. He was only a month old but he was already really big. We both fell in love with him at first sight so Rufus was an immediate new member of our family. As the weeks went by, he would sometimes go into a room and as he walked back by us he would 'yelp' and look a lot bigger, even in only a couple of days. It didn't take him very long to get to his full 85 pound weight and beautiful gray and white haired body. But he also required a lot of care brushing and clipping. He didn't seem to be as smart as Shabam though. With his hair over his eyes he'd run and hit a tree and just fall down, bark, shake himself off and keep running. Shabam and Rufus played well together with Rufus running fast right under Shabam. One day he got too big to do that and flipped Shabam in the air. She turned and growled at him and that was the last time he ever did that but he looked at her like.."duuh! Wha'd I do?" I grew to love Rufus more and more, taking him for rides in my little sports car. One day though, I needed to take Stan's big old car to Karen's house. I left Rufus in the car for just a bit and knocked on her door. "Why did you knock and then leave?" Karen asked with a really confused look on her face. "What are you talking about" I answered with equal confusion, "I just got here"! "Look" Karen said with a voice of authority, "about five minutes ago there was a knock on my door and you yelled your name.....I know your voice real good Judy!....and when I opened the door no one was there, it freaked me out....then I heard another knock on the door and it's you!...are you just playin' games with me?" Karen looked relieved to see me and her face turned to a smile. "No, honest, I just got here" I said, looking more confused than ever. Nodding her head she responded "Well, I guess your spirit got here before you huh?" After laughing over the situation, I settled down enough to explain my visit. "Karen, I just came by to drop these clothes off, can't stay long, Rufus is in the car, and I don't like leaving him alone too long.

When Rufus spotted me he began barking and jumping all over the inside of the car. Unlike Shabam's bark which was much more like squealing, his bark was a repetitious ARF, ARF, ARF which made him all the more unique. As I opened the door, I couldn't believe what I saw. He had tried to get out of the car and had chewed all around the pull up door locks and a lot of the leather on the back of the front seat as well as around the inside of some of the doors. The car looked like it had been in a war zone. "Oh my God Rufus, what did you do? Did something spook you out or what?" I was shocked; I never had a problem with him like this before or with Shabam for that matter. What will Stan say when he sees the damage? Rufus knew he did something wrong and immediately laid down on the seat with his head hangin' down. When we arrived home, Stan saw the car and felt sick. This was our main source of transportation and now it looked like a piece of junk! I tried to describe the incident about the knock on Karen's door to Stan and about Rufus but we had no explanation about it at all. "But Stan", what about Karen hearing my voice? How could that be?" "I don't know hon", Stan replied with a real strange look on his face. "Remember the time I told you about when that real estate man's wife claimed I had called her on the phone and had made some sexual remarks to her? When I checked on the time she said I called, I was having my hair cut during that time. I even had my barber as a witness but that didn't make any difference, she swore it was my voice. The real estate guy got really mad at me and didn't know who to believe, but the matter finally got shoved under the rug. Now this with Karen, what in the world is going on Judy?" Denny knew about that real estate guy's wife accusation....he just blew it off...I don't think he could handle it. Even Harry, my former manager said that maybe we should see a Psychic to find out; he said it sounded like an evil spirit or something! You know, when we went to see that Psychic Reader Lady and I asked her about that incident, she couldn't answer me and she said she'd call me later, but she never did. "Oh yeah Stan, I remember. Oooooh...it all sounds so freaky doesn't it?"

"Gee", I thought, "we've been in this house for over a year now, it's hard to believe". I loved the warm summer months. Stan did too but he was the one to have to cut the acre plus lawn with just a push power mower. But the kids really enjoyed that time of year. Steve and Elliot were able to spend a lot of the summer weeks with us and Kurt and Holly got along with them really good. Kurt and Steven became real buddies only being a year and a half in age difference. They loved playing together, investigating the huge property and building things. Holly and Elliot were much younger but found friendship and other projects with each other as well. "Stan! What are the boys building now?" "I think it's going to be a tree fort babe, they'll probably do a better job at it than I can" Stan answered as he sat comfortably at the kitchen counter with a small glass of wine he was sipping. I loved watching them work and the knowledge the two little young guys had. They searched out all the excess lumber they found in the barn and around the property. Stan had some tools and hardware available, so they had hammers and plenty of nails on hand. It was a little harder for Holly and Elliot to join in. They were also about a year and a half apart in age and a couple of years younger than the boys. Holly was so girlie-girlie and Elliot didn't really want to do girlie stuff so they would usually compromise and ride bikes together and help bring the boys lumber and tools. "Mommy, mommy", Holly came running in the house crying. "Holly, slow down, tell me what's wrong". Holly was always very dramatic in just about anything she said or did. "Mommy, the boys won't let me hang curtains in the fort. I helped too and I want to decorate it". I really had to hold back my laughter. I could just picture the boy's fort looking fussy with curtains. "Holly" I said, in as loving a way as I could, "I know you want to decorate it but the boys want their fort to be boyish, not pretty". It took a while to calm her down but she certainly didn't forget the issue.

The fort was finally finished and Stan and I climbed up the tree to inspect it to make sure it was safe, and it really was....it was amazing at that. "Boys, we are so proud of you both, you did such a great job". "Mom, we all want to sleep out here in the fort tonight". Their faces were lit up with excitement at the thought of it and they were very determined to do just that. "But hey you guys, it's so dark out here at night by the woods, I'm not sure of this", I responded quickly. "Oh Judy", Stan butted in, "they're boys, they'll be fine, they're pretty close to the house anyway. Give them a lot of flashlights. Shabam will stay outside. They'll all have a great adventure". Elliot started to hold his stomach and whimper, "Hey Dad, I want to sleep in there too and Holly helped too...how about us?" Holly looked like a drama was about to happen so we agreed. The boys weren't too happy about the situation but Stan and I felt better about all four of them being together although we knew that Holly and Elliot would probably not stay there the whole night. I wondered what kind of night's sleep I would get. Stan slept through just about everything anyway. We brought out blankets, pillows and, of course, lots of food. It was early evening and dark out as Stan and I sat nervously sipping some wine at the kitchen table. We just waited for Elliot and Holly to come back in the house. They weren't as brave or brazen as the boys. It was about 11 O'clock and I kept peeking out the window and the next thing I saw was all four flashlights running across the lawn and four little voices screaming. As I opened the door, each one came barreling in. "What's going on you guys?....bear try to climb up the tree or what?" They all spoke at once with a lot of fear in their voices. "Ok, one at a time!" Kurt spoke up first. "Mom! Did you and Stan come out to play a trick on us?" "Kurt", I said trying to reassure him, "we just opened the door to check on you but no we weren't anywhere near the fort, why do you think that?" "Mom, if it wasn't you or Stan than who was it?" "Kurt, what are you talking about?" Steven broke in. "Dad, Dad, Jude, the floorboards kept going up and down, we thought it was you playing a trick on us. We kept yelling your names, peeked out the door and window and didn't see anyone; it felt like someone was underneath the fort pushing up on the floor. Even Shabam was barking, we all got scared and decided to come back in...didn't you hear us?" "Look boys, we'll check it out in the morning, O.K.? let's all get to bed and get some sleep" Stan and I just looked at each other and knew it wasn't the time to discuss it and show any fear to the kids but we could hear them talking about it for hours. Once more, funny stuff was happening without any explanation. The next morning we went outside to check on the fort. I climbed up and Stan pushed on the floor beneath it; we were without any real answers. The boys only played in it during the day after that and no fancy curtains were ever put up. We had a great summer going on bike rides, taking the kids to movies, amusement parks and the beach. The beach and ocean was my absolute favorite place to be. Stan built sand castles and 'curvy' mermaids (his favorite thing to do). We were one big happy family.

(Stan)

"I've been think'n babe", Stan said in an upbeat tone, "remember I said that instead of us always buying our Abalone Jewelry from Charles and Sara, let's just fly down to Mexico and buy it ourselves? Ya know, eliminate the middle man?" "Sounds real exciting Stan, when should we go?" "Ok, I've done a lot more than thinking about it, I searched out a lot of facts about Mexico and the town of Taxco and how to do business down there". "AND", I said, interrupting Stan. "Ok., Ok, Jude you know me by now....I made flight reservations for two weeks from now". "TWO WEEKS? STAN, I have to make plans for the kids, school starts then, and oh yeah the animals, and I have to get a responsible house keeper for the kids. and...how 'bout the Cub Scout Webelo troop you lead every week?" "Oh c'mon Jude, stop worrying, we'll work it all out, besides, the airfares are not refundable so get your act together, we're definitely flyin' to Mexico". "Is it alright to ask you how long we'll be away? I mean, I hate to question you.... Mr. Rose!" "MR ROSE!.... haven't heard that one before....uh oh...you sound a little up tight babe, you mad?" "No, just wish you'd start consulting me a little more, before you make all these plans....I just need to be included from now on...O.K.?" "You're right little head, but like I said, non refundable flight tickets. How 'bout the Fudge People...Doug 'n Gale....maybe they'd like to live in a big house in the country for about ten days,... they love the dogs and the kids will be in school every day; they might love to be here, I'd feel real safe with them watching Kurt and Holly." "Don't worry Mr. Rose, I'll take care of it" "There you go again. Wow, you really are pissed off huh babe....O.K., I got the message!" "Oh calm down Stan, I'm just kidding, you know me, I'm real flexible, I'll take care of the details. You just set up all the business we'll have to do in Mexico....hey...you know me, I love spontaneous trips. Remember the time we planned to go to the beach for a weekend and decided at the end of the driveway to go to New York City instead? We packed all the wrong clothes and didn't care". "That's why I fell in love with you sweetheart. You always make life so exciting, so open to new ideas and everything. Ola!...buenos...hasta la vista......can't wait to make love to you Spanish style" "Spanish style? Why Mr. Rose, what DO you have in mind?" "I don't know yet....we need to talk it over...after all...you said you wanted to be included from now on...right? "Tell you what Stan...surprise me...Ok.?" "O.K. doll...whatever you say!"

"Buenos dias Senor, Hable Englais?" I talked as if I knew the language but it was only a few of the words I had learned and hoped the voice at the other end knew my language as well. "Si Senor, what can I help you with?" The English of the guy answering the phone was welcome and surprisingly good and clear considering that it was coming from a hotel in Taxco, a small town in the hills a hundred miles or so north of Mexico City. It kind of had an echo and delay to it but I was relieved that I could communicate my request. It didn't take long to find out that we could have a really nice room at only $6 American in the town's Plaza de la Ciudad, the small round park immediately in front of the hotel. By this time of my life I had let my hair stylist convince me to shape it into an Afro, real popular at the time. During the summer months I had gotten a very dark tan and was even once mistaken at a jewelry show in Chicago for a black guy escorting a white chick around which gave Judy and I a lot of laughs, but I liked my looks and she, as always, let me be me. Arriving at the Mexico City International Airport, I noticed that there were only two or three lines to go through to get to the exit and there was a long line ahead of me. I grabbed our bags and headed for a large column around the whole set up with Jude following me as quickly as she could. "Where are you going Stan, the line is over there?" "No one's looking, quiet hon, just follow me and don't look back". We walked quickly to the outside entrance and hailed a cab. What Judy didn't know was that I had stashed a small amount of marijuana beneath the soap in my shaving dish. I didn't even think of having to go through Mexican Customs before entering the country, dumb move, (what was I thinking, I thought) but, we were clear and on our way to a new adventure. "Wow Judy, Mexico City is like an extra clean New York City, isn't it?" The hotel we were at was located right in the middle of the city and after a short time of investigating some of the sites, we were off to Taxco the following day in a small car driven by a guy who spoke English, but sometimes not too good although he corrected my pronunciation of Taxco to TASCO. The ride was a little 'hairy' going up a lot of winding roads with no guard rails and with a few animal bones scattered here and there, but we arrived finally safe and sound in the quaint little town of Taxco with its circular park in the middle of it. The park like area was spelled Circulo but it sounded more like Zoculo. It had a little band stand in the middle, restaurants all around it including an impressive two story church to one side as well. The Hotel had gorgeous handmade furniture and tiled floors everywhere.

"YOU NEED A TOUR GUIDE SENOR?"

We hadn't even left the lobby when a smallish man with a huge smile approached us from a couch he was sitting on. "My name is Serafin Osorio Ramirez, senor; I can take you wherever you want for a few pesos". "Ok. Serafin, we're here to buy jewelry. We'll only be here for about four or five days" "Stan?" Serafin said with a serious look on his face, "your hair...it is large and sandy colored. Senor, Sandy sounds like Sunday and that is Domingo in Spanish...a good day here...Is O.K. if I call you Domingo?" And Judy is pronounced Hudy in Spanish! (On top of that, our last name being Rose in Spanish was Rosa). 'J's are pronounced as H's so here we were...Stan is Domingo Rosa and Judy is now Hudy on a mountain top in 'ole Mexico! Serafin turned out to be a very trustworthy guide. He took us to Jewelry places where we could really barter for quantities of jewelry and get rock bottom prices. Since we were off for a few days vacationing in Acapulco by bus, he even offered to wait for the jewelry we had ordered to be made and bring it to Mexico City by bus to our hotel, which he did. We saw Charles' and Sara's business card on one of the boards in town where foreigners could pin their cards to and I placed ours arrogantly right next to theirs. It just made me feel equal or superior I guess but it was still underhanded knowing we hadn't told them about our trip. One of the girls in a jewelry factory became fascinated with my afro look and decided I was her Santa Claus. She giggled every time we visited her place of business. Hudy, of course, was an immediate friend of anyone she met there. She was always asking for a lady's room somewhere and in Spanish the name for women is Damas....so....I jokingly began calling her Hudy Damas. Domingo Rosa and Hudy Damas ? ..."Oy Vey, if my Jewish ex friends could only see me now" I thought! The sound of the Mariachi guitarists everywhere and the flavor of the area led to a lot of intimate ecstasy during our off hours while in our small but comfortable hotel suite.

"Hey Jude", I laughed as the bus pulled into town. "LOOK…'Estrella De Oro Bus Lines'……Gold Star Bus Lines? They have to be kidding! Looks more like a 1952 rehabbed bus from the states!" "O.K. Domingo, don't make me laugh, just get on it. It's the only way we're gonna get to Acapulco from here. As we sped down the mountainous roads with no guard rails I could see the cliffs below and prayed we would all make it in one piece. I was sitting next to the window and Hudy couldn't see what I was seeing and as we roared around a curve my window flew wide open with a loud noise and scared me out of my wits. As we finally got to flat roads, the bus stopped and some "Federalies" (Mexican Gov Police) with rifles boarded for inspection. My heart raced at the possibility of them inspecting my luggage and finding the marijuana which Judy still had no knowledge of. We would have spent the rest of our trip in a Mexican Jail if that happened, and besides, we were the only Americanos on the bus, pretty easy to spot but it didn't happen and off we went. It was a Friday night and dark and everyone on the crowded bus was talking Spanish along with some Spanish music playing over scratchy old speakers. On top of that the bus driver was being harassed by some late night drunks on the back of a pickup in front of the bus; the entire trip lasted over four hours. He got mad at one point and kept turning on and off all the headlights and interior lights. The drunks finally turned off and everyone in the bus gave a sigh of relief. We finally arrived late at night in Acapulco and managed to stay at the former glamorous Hilton Hotel now part of the Mexican sector.

"YOU BROUGHT WHAT WITH YOU?" Judy yelled, as she saw me lighting up a joint of the weed I had stashed in my soap dish, "ARE YOU CRAZY? Get rid of that right now, I'm not going to spend my vacation in some Mexican jail." "Ok., O.k. hon", I replied. Knowing she was right, as usual, I went out to our balcony and dumped it in the air almost crying over seeing it all disappear. We did some para sailing (kite flyin' pulled by a long boat line) and nearly got abducted by some really sneaky guys pretending to be the police, looking to fleece us out of our money. Although we were able to see the cliff divers and other sights, we were really happy to fly out of there and get back to the States.

Since we were selling our jewelry everywhere we went, we were wearing a lot of it. I even thought that I would wear a small abalone stone in my ear and even had one ear pierced to show it off. Kurt was totally embarrassed seeing me wearing an earring especially in front of his Webelo troop friends. As I began to unpack all our new jewelry, Judy's voice yelled from another room. "Stan, you'd better call the Webelo Leader of the Cub Scout pack and see how it all went during your absence don't' you think?" "Yeah, you're right, good idea Jude I'll call right now. "Hi Mary, this is Stan can I speak to Bob?" There was complete silence on the other end until Bob's voice suddenly responded, very harsh and very loud. "Look Stan, don't EVER call this house again, you hear me?" "WHAT? why, what's going on" I said, shocked by his tone of voice. The couple had been one of the friendliest people we knew and they were so appreciative of me taking the leadership of the troop when no other fathers had come forward. "YOU CALLED MY WIFE AND SPOKE SEXUAL OBSCENETIES TO HER, THAT'S WHAT!" I couldn't believe what he was talking about. "Bob" I responded, my voice raised a few decibels at the thought of being accused of doing something I couldn't have done even if I wanted to. And besides, with Bob's wife being way overweight as she was, she was definitely not my type and she would have been the last person I would even think of doing that to anyway. "Look, Bob, Judy and I have been out of the country in Mexico for the last 12 days, we just returned today, there's no way I could have called her do you want to see the airline tickets or what?... please put her back on the line!" When Mary reluctantly got back on the phone I explained it all over again to her. Bob's voice suddenly broke in even more firmly than before. "Yup, she says there's no doubt it was you and I believe her so don't ever call here anymore". With that the phone went dead. Hanging up the receiver I stood absolutely stunned by the conversation. This was the third time this had happened to me. A voice, similar or imitating mine had called three different people over the last three years doing the same thing. Once with Judy's babysitter, once with the real estate guy's wife and now with the Webelo Leader's wife. "JUDE", I yelled with absolute panic in my voice.

WHAT THE HELL'S GOING ON!"

(Judy)

Man, it feels good to be back in America. I never realized what a great country we live in until you leave it. It was the longest time I was ever away and I was never so happy to see the children. Doug and Gail, our 'fudge people' friends, were wonderful with them. Everyone was so excited to see all the jewelry we had bought, it sure was an exciting business. "I was married to Joe for 9 years and hardly ever went out, now look at me", I thought. I'm traveling everywhere, New York, Chicago, Mexico! "SAJA IMPORTS" "My gosh Stan, it's really our business. I know we sold jewelry before, but this trip made it so real" "Yeah hon, it certainly is, and you ain't seen nothin' yet!" The business really took off. We were selling jewelry everywhere but we still favored the mamma & pop stores the most. The catalog helped a lot as we were able to mail out the items they ordered from it. I couldn't get the incident with Mary, the Webelo Leader's wife, out of my mind and it started playing funny tricks on me. It was too unusual to say the least. I remembered the last two incidents with Stan's real estate friend's wife saying he called and then the babysitter in my apartment, and now this; my mind really started racing. Could it be true? But how? Mary said she received the call and heard his voice and knew for sure it was Stan. But we were in Mexico at that time, it was impossible and besides, she was definitely not a woman Stan would ever be interested in. My babysitter swore that it was Stan's voice and that he had made filthy remarks to her too. "You know Stan I have to say, this is really troubling me, what's this all about?" "Judy, I'm really confused. Is someone trying to destroy my character or split us up or what? You know I was with you 24 hours a day in Mexico, besides, a call from there sounds like it's inside a garbage can....pretty obvious it's not from here". "I know Stan but how could anyone imitate your voice like that, all those people swore it was you!" "Judy you know me, I NEVER called any of those women, I swear to you and oh yeah... how 'bout the time your voice was heard at Karen's house? Remember that?" "Stan, I believe you but I just don't know what to make of the whole thing". "You know Jude, I've been thinking, is this what they call a spirit?" " A WHAT? What's a 'spirit'? Now you're really scaring me Stan". "Well, you know, like I heard that spirits can imitate things, even appear sometimes". "O.K., let's not go there Stan, drop it for now". A week went by and we had to attend a Webelo meeting at the school and Stan brought our plane tickets to show Bob and Mary to prove where we were but they were not interested. Bob still believed his wife and that was that. I looked over at Mary and she looked at me and I knew that my Stan could never have called her. My thoughts were going wild. It kept ringing over and over again; maybe there is such a thing as a spirit world. I started remembering what had happened at Karen's house when she heard the knock on her door with no one there and she hearing my voice too… it was all too freaky. I just wanted to put it all behind me.

Most Saturday nights and all day Sunday, Kurt and Holly would be with their Dad so it gave Stan and I a little time alone. We decided to forget it all and go dancing with Ken and Lin. Den and Jack surprised us and decided to join us as well. The evening was wonderful. We stayed out till 2 am, danced, partied, had a ball. I tried to sleep late but Shabam and Rufus needed to go out. As I walked down the stairs there was that stupid troll with its red eyes staring at me. I hated that thing but I didn't want to tell Stan. He liked to sleep late so I decided to go for a walk on our path through the woods with the dogs. I loved this property and I hoped that we could buy it someday. It was more than I could ever dream of. Fall was in the air and it was beginning to get nippy outside. I walked near the small cemetery to read the names and dates on some of the stones still standing. 1830, 1860, 1875, wow! These people were dead a long time. It was sad to see the children's head stones; some of them had such a short life. It seemed as though you either made it to a ripe old age or died really young not much in between. I thought about Kurt and Holly and Stan's boys and knew we were so lucky to have such healthy kids. I walked a little further with the dogs who were playing and running ahead of me and then down to the little pond where the kids skated in the winter months, it was so peaceful. I knew I'd better get back before Stan woke up, he'll wonder where I disappeared to. When I got back, Stan was still sleeping. God, I hated him sleeping so late and I knew it was from all the pot he was smoking before he went to bed. I decided to wake him up but in a loving way or otherwise he'd get good and angry. Jack and Dennis came back to the house and we spent a fun day with them waiting for Kurt and Holly to return home. As Joe pulled up to the house I went out to say hello to him but he was always very cool to me but I felt a little sad for him, he looked so lonely. "Hi kids, did you have fun? "Mom, look at all the presents dad bought us". "Wow, you both have your hands full, let's get you inside". I looked over at Stan and saw his face and what he was thinking. $37.50 a week for child support for each kid and he showers them with gifts like a real hero! I had to agree but I never had the guts to fight him for more child support and Stan still fumed over it.

"Hey Kurt, what's this thing?" "Oh, mom, it's called a Ouija Board, it's really cool, it can do magical things, wanna try it?" "Maybe after dinner Ok?" The kids already ate so I fixed dinner for Jack, Dennis me and Stan and sent the kids upstairs to play with their new toys. Afterwards, Kurt brought the Ouija Board down and we all sat around it. "My dad said all you have to do is put one hand lightly on the plastic pointer, ask it a question and it will move around to the letters and spell out the answer", Kurt said excitedly. "Mom, ask it a question, see what happens!" "Mmmmm, what should I ask, Ok., what color is my car?" Nothing happened for a few seconds and then all of a sudden even though my hand was just resting on it, it moved all around the board. First to the letter Y, then to the E, then L, L again and then O and W. "Whoa, this is freaky", I said as I jerked my hand away from it. "Jackie, you try it...go ahead!" "How'd it know that?" Jackie said with a cynical smirk, "you moved it didn't you Jude?" "No, honest Jackie, I really didn't!" "Ok., Uh...what's my dog's name Ouija?" "Jackie" I said, "put your hand on it very lightly!" "I am Jude, what d'ya think I'm doin?.. what the frig is goin' on...this thing is moving everywhere.....W H A A T ?... it just spelled out PUNZONE...how did this piece of plastic and cardboard know that? It's freakin' me out!" We were all laughing and must have looked so silly and surprised as we asked it one question after another with this thing coming up with perfect answers. We finally exhausted ourselves and put the board away.

78

It was the most intriguing thing I had ever seen. "I'm leaving this funny house", Jackie said, half laughing, "Better not see a witch flyin on a broom outside", still laughing and half snippy as she usually did. After she and Den left, the kids and us continued to laugh about the whole time we just had together.

"Stan, how did this thing know all the answers like that?" "Good question Freckles, who knows, maybe it can read our minds huh? I aint got a clue. Honey it's just a silly board game, forget it". Stan said that but my mind wanted to know more, it answered too many questions correctly. "Hey Stan, maybe we can ask the Ouija what happened in this house throughout the years, you know? If only the walls could talk as they say". "Oh yeah...what do you think the walls would say Jude?" "Oh, I don't know, maybe it would be fun to find out the history of the house, it's very old and a lot of people lived here. We know a mafia guy who lived here. Remember those guys with the guns who came looking for that guy Joel?" "O.K. hon, someday we'll investigate it but let's go to bed now. As I lay awake, all I could think about was the Ouija Board.

(Stan)

"Hi...You want to buy my Jewelry senor?" As we were admiring our display of jewelry at a nearby indoor Flee Market we were part of, we looked up startled to see a smiley faced young gal speaking English with a decidedly Spanish flavor. "Hi", she said again, "my name is Alicia, just call me Alice". "Well hi there Alice, I'm Stan and this is Judy, whad'ya got in that big bag of yours?" "I am a student and I sell beautiful handmade turquoise jewelry. I see by your signage on the Mexican made blanket it says FLEE TO MEXICO...so you import all this 'las joyas' senor? It is so unusual, sterling and abalone shell is the rage now". Alice just kept staring at all of the displays as she answered back in her cute and funny way, occasionally chuckling and adding a Spanish accent to her speech. Hardly resisting the impulse after hearing the words 'las joyas' (or jewelry in Spanish) and the way she accented the J in joyas with a guttural H), I asked "are you Spanish?" "No Stan, I am Italian! There, I'll drop the Spanish accent....O.K., I've just been admiring the two of you as you've been selling here, and you both look like you have so much fun together". "Well yes we do, and I'd love to buy some of your jewelry Alice but our friend Ken is also selling turquoise here and we don't want to be his competition…..but look, you seem like a very honest hard working student, a few rings and maybe a bracelet or earrings wouldn't hurt, what do you think Jude?" "Ok. Stan, her turquoise is completely different from anything Ken has; I think it would be alright, besides, I like you Alice, you look like so much fun". "YOU WILL?" she answered. Her face lit up like a child having a request for candy answered with a yes! Somehow I knew that we had just made another valuable contact. What I didn't know was that we had just made a permanent friend who would become totally involved with not only our business but our family as well.

The rest of 1976 was filled with shipping our goods to several different places during a hectic selling just period prior to the upcoming holidays. We'd also get up real early on a Sunday morning in some fairly cold weather and sell at retail what we could in outside flee markets. As Christmas drew closer, we were also searching other booths for gifts for our kids and friends. We found lots of bargains but not everything we were looking for. Smitty and his wife, who had become one of our closest friends, were a challenge to buy anything for. They were a very intelligent couple and we would often get together to play Scrabble and other challenging board games with. "Ya know Jude, I really think they would get a big laugh out of one of those witchcraft starter potion kits we saw down at the Flaming Cauldron, wha d'ya think?" "Hmmm, I don't know Stan I still feel freaky going in that store around that strange lady, but, Ok., it's just a joke anyway…we'll just include it with that new game we bought them". "Hey hon, the real surprise will be the starter potion kit and if I know Smitty, he'll use it too. Maybe he'll make himself into a real Leprechaun, ya think?" "O.K. Stan, enough of that, I have the chills just thinking about it!"

Chapter 6

DARK DAYS

"Finally hon, Christmas morning! and look at it...isn't it all absolutely beautiful outside...everything is so pure white with the sunlight shining through the trees?" "Yes Stan and I can't wait to go out there later with the kids and the dogs". Stevie and Elliot had stayed with us for a few days so we had all four children with us that morning. They all came running down the stairs at once ready to open presents, hardly getting out of the way of each other. "Whoa, hold on you guys, we're going to have a small breakfast before we go into the living room Ok".? Their little faces full of excitement calmed down a bit as we sat down for the short meal. Just as we were about to leave the kitchen, we all heard strange sounds going on outside.

"CLANG, CLANG, CLANG!". The sound of bells was heard loud and clear and coming from our barn in back of the house. The only problem was that there weren't any bells anywhere in the barn. "Where are those bells coming from Mom? Hey Steven, hurry up let's go open presents and we'll go investigate it ...Ok.?" Kurt yelled. Stan and I looked at each other in total amazement as the children ran into the living room. Stan leaned over and whispered, "Ya think Smitty had anything to do with this Jude?" I looked at him with a blank stare and didn't respond, after all it was Christmas morning and I didn't want anything to ruin the fun. "Slow down boys, we're going to be here for a while, there's plenty of time to go out and look around for the bells, and hey maybe one of Santa Claus' reindeer got caught up in the top floor of the Barn!" The kids all had a good laugh but I could see they were really intrigued at the thought of what they might find in the barn. We all had a great time opening our presents following our tradition of each person opening their gift while the others waited so everyone could enjoy the fun. We lit a fire, had hot chocolates and a lot of laughs. The boys couldn't wait to get outside and investigate the strange sounds coming from the barn. "Mom", yelled Kurt, "Can we go now? We want to see what's clanging in the barn". "Ok, go ahead boys, let us know what you find". Holly and Elliot wanted to tag along as well so Stan and I watched from the window smiling at each other as we watched the kids running around in total excitement over what they thought they might find. I didn't know how Stan was feeling but I was sure curious. Could it be that it was really done through that starter witchcraft set we gave Smitty or what? "Stan, what the hell's going on here? How could a stupid little board game or some dumb potion thing cause spells on things?" Stan just looked at me with the most puzzled look I had ever seen on him. We decided at that moment to go out and check the barn ourselves but found nothing even though we kept hearing the sounds of bells. As the children and Stan were walking all through the barn I decided to go in and call Smitty.

"Hey Smitty, Merry Christmas; what are you and Charlee up to? Did you both enjoy the fun gift we sent you?" "Que pasa Jude? why do you ask? somethin' strange goin' on over there?" "Yeah, you might say that. Stan and the kids are still outside running all over the place trying to find out where the bells are ringing in the barn. We thought you and Charlee might be playing around with that potion thing we sent you, but c'mon, that stupid witchcraft set can't create anything right?" "Oh Jude, lighten up, we just mixed up a potion and sent a friendly spirit to your house". Smitty chuckled and I could also hear Charlee laughing in the background. "Just think Jude, this is so cool, hey if we mixed a potion and it can ring bells in your barn I wonder what else it can do"? "Oh sure you guys I can just imagine what you two could think up knowing the two of you. Look Smitty just don't turn yourself into a Leprechaun Ok.? See ya later".After hanging up the phone I got chills that ran right through me. This whole situation freaked me out, but eventually the bells stopped ringing and we all just enjoyed the rest of Christmas day with a lot of our friends dropping by. We had worked hard before the holidays and sold a lot of jewelry and we were making our plans for the New Year. A few strange things were beginning to happen in the house but we just tried to ignore it.

Another trip to Mexico was necessary to replenish our inventory. Our friends Ken and Linda wanted to join us so we all booked our flights together. They had their parents to watch their boys and we got Alicia and her mom Vicky to watch Kurt and Holly. We knew what to expect on the road from Mexico City to the mountain town of Taxco but Linda freaked out on the curves and felt real sick. She just about fell out of the small van as we arrived in the town She recovered quickly though and we all had a fun time shopping all over for our jewelry, us for the Abalone and them for their turquoise and leather goods. It felt real good having our friends with us as our guide Serafin took us around to a lot of new places to buy. This trip also opened up a lot of new suppliers for us.

"STAN!" "What's the matter Jude, you don't look so good, you feeling all right babe?" "I don't know hon, I just feel nauseous, ache all over, I have to lie down". "Jude, you look white as a sheet, better get you back to the hotel room for a while". Soon after getting into the room I began to heave all over the place. I felt like dying at that point, even when a small roach walked across my foot, I could've cared less. "Jude, look, we only have today left to buy our stuff. I'll go get a doctor and then I'll go finish up our buying spree". Stan went to the other side of the town "Zocolo" to the doctor's office. He told me later that the doctor shut down the office and drove about two blocks in one of the few cars in town to the hotel. He said they could've walked the distance faster but the doc was used to treating a lot of us crazy Americanos and was in no rush and besides, it was impressive to drive his car instead of walking. He took one look at me and wanted to put me in the hospital. "Are you crazy" I moaned, "NO HOSPITAL"...you give me medicine...SI?" "Ok, Si Senora", he answered. "Senor, you go to the store and have this prescription filled quickly. I'll stay here with the Senora until you return". Stan looked at me in bewilderment not knowing what to do. Was this guy really a doctor or what? Too weak to argue I responded, "Go honey, I'll be fine". I could feel Stan's panic as he left the room. I just laid there moaning and groaning with a totally strange "so called" doctor looking at me. I figured if he was going to molest or rape me he then good luck to him, he'd be a mess. As it turned out, he really was concerned about my recovery only. Stan flew through the door with a small bag in hand. "Gracias", said the doc, "do you have any alcohol handy Senor, I need this to give the Senora the medicine with the needle"."NO I DON'T....DON'T

YOU?" Stan said getting more upset by the minute. "Senor, you have after shave or something?" Stan grabbed his Old Spice and the doctor poured it over the needle and gave me a shot right in my butt and then left some additional medicine to take orally later. We thanked him, paid a simple fee of $25 and he was on his way. I couldn't believe that within two hours I was walking around feeling almost normal. "Whatever he did really worked fast but the only thing is Stan is that I have quite a lump in my butt from the old spice". "Yeah, but just think how good your cute little butt will smell now", he replied. We both had a good laugh about it all and tried to figure out what had made me so sick. I had learned to ask for "Aqua Purificado" (purified water) to drink in the hotel but hadn't realized that just taking a shower or using the wrong faucet for brushing my teeth could make you sick. Stan wasn't affected by it for some reason. The town folks had acquired immunity to the bad water from birth so it didn't really bother them either very much.

Well, in spite of everything that happened, we got to purchase what we needed and were really happy to get back home at last. Kurt and Holly ran to the car. They seemed very relieved more than ever that we were home. We found out that Alicia's mother Vicky had a mini stroke and had to go to the hospital the day before. The only problem was that Alicia had to take her there and had left the children alone and stayed with her mom overnight. They were way too young to be left alone and I was torn between being really upset with Alicia but also concerned for her mom. Kurt and Holly were still a little freaked out and unsettled over the whole experience. "Kids, where was Desi during all of this?" I asked, suddenly realizing that she had been my permanent backup for anything like this happening to my kids. "Oh, she went to visit her friend's house for a couple of days. Mommy, we were scared, we heard all kinds of noises in the house". "Kurt, I'm so proud of you, you took care of your sister. I'm not happy you were left alone and it won't ever happen again." "Mom, please don't ever have Alicia's mom be with us anymore. She woke us up every morning by standing at our bedroom door and banging pots and pans!" I could feel my blood boiling but I didn't want to make any more of it in front of the children so I just made a joke of it. They both clung to me and for the next few days I could feel their insecurity. Desi finally came home a day later and I explained what happened. "DESI?" where did you go, you were supposed to stay here and help Alicia and her mom?' "UH, Jude, my friend Susan asked me over for a few days, hey look, Mrs. Petrillo drove me crazy with her pots and pans and her yelling all the time so I decided to stay with my friend for a few days, I figured the kids would be alright". "I'm sorry everyone, I thought Alicia and her mom would be fun, they won't be house sitting again don't worry".

(Stan)

"JUDY!...did you hear that?" "Hear what?" "The voices and music playing downstairs!" Stan whispered as he shut our bedroom door one night. "Every time I open the door a little I can hear it, then it goes away real fast". "C'mon Stan, you're just messin' with me right?" "No hon, honest, it's kind of quiet noise but it's real!" As Stan opened the door quietly again, he saw Desi running up the stairs shaking. "STAN, JUDE, I was downstairs letting Rufus out cause he was starting to bark and I saw the wall phone floating in the air....I'm freakin' out...what's goin' on here?" "I dunno Desi, forget it, go to bed we'll talk about it in the morning. "Jude, ya think Smitty and Charlee are up to their tricks again?' "I don't know Stan, but if they are, they better cut it out, or I'm going to go over there and take that potion kit away from them." "O.K Jude, I'll call them in the morning"

"SMITTY!... Hey you little Leprechaun". "Que Pasa Stan...wha's up my friend?" "Smitty, you and Charlee been up to your tricks again with that silly potion thing we gave you?" "Us? Now Stan, what would ever make you think that?" "Right Smitty, you damn well know why I would think that, especially with your sense of humor, you and Charlee that is, you're both the same". "Aaww, Stan, I'm really hurt to think you think that about me!" (Smitty's muffled laughter on the other end got me goin' as well).. There's no way anyone could ever stay mad at this guy, I certainly couldn't that was for sure. "Hey look Stan, really, Charlee and I were out of town visiting her folks, we only did that one thing we told you about, honest!...why, What's going on?" "Oh just some strange things pal, when you and Charlee visit we'll tell you all about it". Judy looked at me with a look of expectation that Smitty and Charlee were the culprits of all the funny noises goin' on but of course that didn't explain the floating phone receiver in the air that Desi said she saw...but then, Desi could be very over dramatic anyway and hard to believe. "What did Smitty say Stan?" "Nothing really hon, I think he's telling the truth. Said he and Charlee were away visiting her folks and swore they hadn't touched the potion kit since Christmas. So much for that, let's just all settle down, I think we're all just letting our imaginations get the best of us". (*Deep down though, my spirit was very unsettled over the whole experience and I couldn't help feeling that we were all getting involved in a world we didn't belong in, like a veil of darkness surrounding us*).

"Hey Jude, I think Ken and Lin just drove up". As I went outside to greet them, I couldn't help noticing the panic on their faces. "What's wrong you guys, you look a little pale....you and the kids Ok," Ken answered with an obvious shaking in his voice. "No Stan, everything's not O.K. Lin's dad is missing again....you know, remember we told you that he sometimes just walks out of the house and disappears for a while, well this time it's been two days and Lin and her mom are really worried. We don't know why, it seemed to start when he hit his 40's but he's now in his 50's." "Gee, I don't know what to say, what we can do to help?" Just then Judy came down from upstairs and joined the conversation. "Linda, why do you think your dad keeps doing this?" "I don't know Judy, I thought it was just a mid life crisis or something, but he's way past that and still acting strange". "Hmmm, hey, this may sound really bizarre, but remember what we were telling you about the Ouija Board telling us stuff that was always true? Maybe we could ask it where your dad is, who knows, maybe we can find him that way". "Lin looked at Ken quizzically then back at us. "Hey let's give it a try, what can we lose right?" "Oh God", replied Ken, this is getting real freaky but O.K., bring it on bro!"

"OUIJA", I said in a commanding voice, "FIND LINDA'S DAD!". Linda placed her hand on the pointer lightly and after a few seconds it started to move as it spelled out letters and numbers on the board. **R T E 4 4 S T A R L I T E B A R** "Did you all see that", Ken yelled, "LET'S GO THERE!" "Hold on Ken, you sure 'bout that? That's about 35 minutes from here way down south in the middle of nowhere" "Yeah, who cares, you guys coming with us O.K.?" There was no stopping Ken when he made up his mind and after thinking about it, Judy and I loved spontaneous trips, long or short. Besides all that Ken always had a small stash of some pretty good weed to smoke so at the very least, we'd have a party on the way. "**Desi**" I yelled as I was closing the door, "watch the kids, we'll be home in a couple of hours....**DESI?...you there?**" "YEAH, I'm upstairs; I'll watch 'em". I wished I had felt better about leaving her in charge since our last experience when we were in Mexico. She was hitting that funny teen age time. Her head was often up in the clouds with music by KISS and boys in general. The trip went much faster than expected. By this time night had set in and finding the Bar wasn't as easy as we expected but its lights lit up the darkness. As we pulled into the parking lot of the small one story cheesy looking building we saw Linda's dad's Lincoln parked directly in front of the entrance. It was easy to spot as it was only one of three or four cars in the entire parking lot. "**WHOA**", Ken yelled, look at that, the OUIJA Board led us right to him; we'd have never found him way out here!" We were all stunned and relieved at the same time to see Lin's dad sitting in his car at that very moment. Talking to him about his whereabouts was a blur to him. He didn't have the strangest idea of why or how he got to the Bar or how much time had passed. Linda drove her dad back to her mom's house and Ken took Judy and me home. As we came down to reality from smoking a small amount of marijuana, our conversation about the whole experience went from hysterical laughter to serious questions about Lin's dad's mental state but the location of the motel spelled out by the OUIJA Board could not be denied and that occupied most of our discussion during the ride home. Our curiosity about the 'unknown' had definitely taken us to another level. The *'Veil of Deceit'* took its serious hold on Judy and me and although Ken and Lin joked about it after that they appeared nervous and never really wanted to talk about it much. The worst part of it was that they, as well as some of our friends, began to see us as 'funny' and 'strange' and didn't feel totally comfortable when visiting us in the house.

(Judy)

"Ya know Stan, I really hate winter, I'm a sun person, I love flowers and green things, its white and pretty now but it's soooo 'dead' lookin'. **STAN! Will you get out of bed already!......**it's almost noon". "Frig you Judith, I'm not in bed I'm in the bathroom, don't get your panties twisted, I'll be down soon!" "Oh, so now you're swearing at me well frig you too buddy! We have a business to run and you smoke so much pot, you can't get up in the morning....hurry up will ya!" I didn't quite understand my impatience with Stan 'cause a lot of times in the past I had joined him in love making in the morning but lately my moods seemed to change from day to day....sometimes from hour to hour. Stan often looked at me with amazement as I walked out of a room in one mood and walked back in a totally different personality. His famous words were always, *"who are you and what have you done with Judy?"* I often wondered the same thing about myself. I sometimes flared up so badly that I would wind up hiding in closets to avoid Stan's yelling and screaming at me or I would simply jump in my little sports car and take off for parts unknown for hours on end. He had also begun to behave strangely by throwing things. Once he even pulled a kitchen drawer out full of silverware in frustration and it landed all over the floor. As peaceful as it usually was, I could swear there was a 'presence' directly behind me or even in front of me. We were living a strange new existence but our love for each other was always what we clung to.

It was a weekend and Stan's boys were visiting. They always looked forward to the weekend because they were living at their grandmother's house after Stan had lost all of his properties. "Hey guys, why don't you go outside and play for a while?; but first let me fix you all a big breakfast". "Yea" they all screamed at once, "I want pancakes", "I want French toast" "I just want cereal"!! "O.K., calm down, you know if you all help we can make it all and everyone can share, how 'bout that?" They all loved helping me out and it was such a fun time of day. I began to fume more and more with Stan sleeping so late, getting up then going back to bed, especially since he was missing all the fun with his boys so I decided to blast the stereo with some really loud music and party in the kitchen with the kids hoping he would get up on his own. I couldn't believe he could sleep through all that noise but he did. I got tired of being so passionate and going up all the time and kissing him that I decided enough was enough. If I'm up with all the children then he better get his lazy butt up and stay up already. I felt this anger coming up inside me knowing an argument was about to happen but I couldn't control myself. I stormed in the bedroom and started slamming things around. "What the hell are you .doing Judy?" Stan groaned. "Well it's about time you got up, you were up and went back to bed. We already had breakfast, kids got ready and they're all outside waiting for you, so get up already!" Stan was about to blow, big time! He hated being woken up like that but I kept needling him. I wanted to be loving like usual but I couldn't. "Oh my God, why did I just do that?"...now he's really ticked off! When Stan got mad he wouldn't stop yelling. He'd storm away and then come back ten seconds later and just keep going on and on, sometimes following me all over the place. I couldn't stand one more minute of his foul language on top of all the yelling so I left him alone and went outside with the kids. About an hour and a half later, he finally got ready and wanted breakfast. Here it was noon and he wants breakfast. "Shove it up your butt sweetheart", I answered. Boy, did I feel bitchy that day

(What was this 'force' driving me to react so completely different than I had always been used to? It wasn't me...or was it?...well, whatever it was it sure felt good!)

I loved Stan so much so why am I such a bitch to him today? I catered to my ex husband and look where it got me. No man will ever control me again, I thought. I'm going to keep my new independence no matter what. By then the kids all came running back into the house. Stan was still eating some cereal he poured and I didn't want to fight in front of the kids so I put on my happy face and made everyone lunch, even Stan, .but...with a few 'sly' remarks slipping out of me. I didn't want to ruin the while day so I gave Stan a big kiss. That was my way of saying 'sorry'. I had a hard time expressing it any other way but he knew me and the rest of the day turned out great.

"Hey Stan, It's been a long day how 'bout running down to Smitty's new bar & grille in town?" "Yeah Jude, sounds great, I'll call Den & Jackie maybe they can join us; you get the kids situated for the night". "Desi, Stan and I are going out for a few hours so you're in charge". Desi rolled her eyes at me like most teenagers do when they are told or asked to do something they could care less about. "Ok, Judy but would it be all right if I invited my friend Patsy over?" "Well yes but you make darn sure that the two of you keep track of the kids and get them into bed by ten". "No problem" she answered in her flippant way, but deep down I always felt slightly less assured of her promises and never 100 per cent at ease leaving the children alone under her supervision. But, partying with Stan and our friends always took preference over just about anything else we were doing at the time. We met a lot of friends at the bar we hadn't seen in a while. Den and Jack showed up soon after we arrived and with a lot of our friends all in one place we had a wild evening filled with laughter and fun. We did however, decide to be more responsible with our hours away from home and cut the night short. When we pulled in the driveway behind the house Desi and her friend came running out with a frightened look on their faces. "What's up Des, the kids O.K.?" "Yeah, yeah" she blurted, they're fine. Patsy and I were just now in the living room when you drove up and we were talking about the weird stuff that goes on in the house when all of a sudden we heard this loud noise coming from the basement. It sounded like an explosion, the whole house shook". The kids were standing in the kitchen as we ran into the house and opened the cellar door. "WHOA" Stan said nervously, he never reacted calmly to emergencies so I knew something was terribly wrong, or so I thought. "What the frig, hey Jude, it looks like a fireball down there but I don't smell any smoke". Stan and I went slowly down the stairs with the kids, Desi and her friend Patsy were just watching from above. The whole basement was lit up from the glow from a real fire. "STAN WHAT IS IT?" I shouted from the bottom of the stairs, still a little scared of following him any closer. "WHAT IN THE WORLD?" Stan yelled back, "The door to the furnace is completely open exposing the fire and that's what's reflecting the red color all over the place! Judy, there's no way this door could have blown open. It has a really strong latch on it". Stan had to get something to push the hot door shut. After settling down, we both realized that the latch was so heavy and strong that it could never have gotten released all by itself. When the door opened, it had hit a pipe on the wall and that's what shook the house. We knew that the children would never go near the furnace and Desi would never even go down into the basement at all. There were times when any of us were down there that as we walked back up the stairs it felt like someone was right behind us with a knife or something....it always gave us the chills. Even Stan never went down there much unless he had to check a fuse or get into the huge safe he had moved there from his office. We just all looked at each other in bewilderment and Stan made a joke about it to calm everyone down (including himself!). We had no other words to say. We all loved this home but there were unexplainable things happening. "Come on guys" I said quietly, "let's just all go to bed and put this behind us. "Yeah" Stan said real convincingly, "I probably just forgot to latch the furnace door shut completely".

"Stan thanks for that", I said, relieved to see everyone back to normal. "I don't want any of them to worry or be frightened. Do you really think that it was just the latch?" "Jude, if you saw how that latch is made, you can't just hook it half way closed or it won't shut at all! I'll tell you one thing, it freaked me out a lot but right now I want to believe what I just told the kids and Desi. Let's just call it a night and go to bed". Just as I was about to fall asleep, there went the soft music again coming from downstairs. I slowly got out of bed so as not to wake up Stan, opened the door slowly to check it out and met Desi in the hallway. We both whispered to each other but I could see the fear on her face. "Judy, where is that music coming from? Every time I open my door the music stops" "I don't know Des, but if Casper the friendly ghost wants to have fun and play music, at least it's entertaining, good night Des". Desi went quickly back into her room, shut her door and put her stereo on softly without another word.

(Stan & Judy)

"Ya know Jude; living in this historic house on this beautiful piece of property is really great. Just standing on the road looking at it is like something you'd see in a movie but so many strange things have been happening. I don't know about you but this furnace door thing shook me up more than the music and the bells. Dramatic as Desi can get, even the floating phone has me half believing her! It's all just too weird. How about that woman you just met, did she say anything about that guy Joel the mafia thugs were looking for? I don't believe in ghosts but I just feel that we're supposed to find out some facts about that guy, don't you? And both of us are acting strange with each other lately, what's goin' on hon?" Sometimes when I'm alone here, I feel like there are eyes watching me. They aren't your gorgeous green eyes babe, that's for sure!" "As a matter of fact Stan, that woman I met, I think her name is Delores, she looked at me very strangely when we talked and she did say some things I've been wanting to tell you about. It's even more crazy my meeting her at all for that matter! She's a friend of Desi's mom Myra. We all went out to lunch and we were having a really fun time but I was beginning to feel a little uncomfortable because she kept staring at my eyes so I finally asked her what's up,…is there something wrong? Stan I didn't like a lot of the things she started to tell me. She asked me a lot of questions about our house". "Our house,..what about our house?...what do you mean Jude? Did Myra say anything to her about some of the strange things happening?" "I don't think so Stan but she said she saw things in my eyes; she started to shake and said "MURDER, MURDER, and LAKE!" "I think she's a Psychic". "Go on babe what else did she say?" "Stan, it scared me and I was afraid to say anything at first in case it was true!" "Come on Jude, it may give us a hint as to what's been happening around here". "Well Ok, let me know what you think. When I asked her what she meant by "murder" …who was murdered? she said that she saw the man who used to live here dropping a woman's body in the pond across the street. I told her then about all the cars that have plowed right into the granite wall on our property in between the pond and the wall and that all the drivers said they saw a woman standing in the middle of the road soaking wet and they tried to avoid her and went into the wall". "Yeah Jude and you know none of them seemed to know what happened to them until later when they could think about it". "Stan, by this time I couldn't even eat my lunch. All I wanted to do was to run because everything she said I believed to be true! Stan look, people who knew this guy Joel…you know…like the mafia with the guns that came looking for him that day, the girl that lived with him disappeared!" "Hon, how'd you know about Joel's girlfriend"? "Ok, a girl I met a few months ago used to go with Joel and knew his girlfriend Sara. Remember Stan? I told you about that!" "Oh yeah, I did forget about it, hey….this is turning into a lot like a mystery novel or something huh? We just have to put together all the pieces". "STAN! This is way too weird for me. That lady Delores wants to come by our house and feel the 'vibes';….what the heck is she talking about?" "Jude, call her, I gotta know more, and this is getting exciting!"

("I don't know about you lover boy" I thought, "but I feel like I'm being drawn into something I'm going to regret"!)

"Boy this makes me nervous Stan, having this stranger come to our house but you're right I really do want to find out what really happened on this property....Oh my God, she's here!" "Look Jude, don't be so nervous will ya, she's just a human being with spiritual powers, relax already this will all be just a lot of fun!" "Oh yeah Stan, it's the spiritual powers that scare me!" "Well babe I'll be by your side, let's see what happens, go let her in...okay?" "Umm..... okay! Hi Delores, this is my husband Stan. "Hi Stan, heard a lot about you!" "That's scary, was it good or bad?" "Oh gee, good of course, Judy had so many beautiful things to tell me about both of you but also a lot about all of the weird stuff going on in your home". "Boy, you got that right. Judy and I want to know anything you can tell us, I understand you have psychic ability, is that true?, I mean I've really never had any belief in any of that but hey, I'm willing to listen". "Stan, that's why I'm here, let's get started".

Delores had a definite "presence" in her looks and dress that was comforting but somewhat creepy at the same time. We watched her closely as she walked through the house, touching everything in sight. She stopped and peered through the living room window at the barn. "Is the barn part of the property Stan?" she asked with an uncomfortable expression on her otherwise plump and cheerful face. "Oh yeah, it sure is". "I need to go into it; I feel that something happened in there". Stan and I followed Delores the short distance to the barn's entrance, looking at each other with a lot of strange expressions as we walked closely behind her. Once inside, she stopped briefly at each empty stall until she came to one and pointed her finger at the wall inside it. "It was here, look", she said with a loud whisper. I looked at Stan in fear as we noticed a large red stain running down one side of the wall. "What's that?" I said loudly, "Please don't tell me what I think it is!" Stan looked at me and Delores and added, "C'mon, that could have been from one of the cows years ago....couldn't it?" "Well, look you guys" Delores responded quickly, "I feel that there was something very evil that happened her; that's not an animal blood stain, I can tell you that for sure". Right then I wanted her to shut up and even go home but yet inside me I knew she was going to tell me a lot more of what I didn't want to know but yet I was still very curious. I was just very glad that the children weren't with us to hear or see this. I didn't want their overactive imaginations and fear get to them. Delores turned to Stan suddenly, "Let's go inside Stan there's something I want you to do". Stan looked at me and shrugged his shoulders. Once inside the house, she handed him a pen and paper and had him sit crossed legged in the middle of our living room floor. "Stan, look, this may really feel weird to you I know, but I feel that the gal that was living here was killed and wants to tell us something. I'm going to sprinkle salt in a circle around you and I want you to close your eyes and just relax while I chant softly. It's called "automatic writing". The female spirit will write through your hands as I pray". As Delores walked quietly around Stan speaking in unfamiliar words, Stan's hand moved slowly and began writing something on the paper he was holding. The writing was definitely not his. It was light and pretty. As I peered over his shoulder from the couch I was sitting on, I started to make out the words that were appearing.

M U R D E R...M U R D E R..... L A K E....M O N E Y...D I G
Stan's eyes snapped open in an instant and he dropped the pen and got quickly up. "What was that about?" he said loudly, "it didn't feel like my hand at all! My hand felt like a small woman's hand, it was light as a feather, I could hardly make the pen write on the paper, in fact I was sure it wasn't writing anything at all" As we all looked at the paper and the words written on it, we knew, that we knew, that we had entered a different spiritual realm and that our lives were about to change directions in some very dramatic ways. "Well, I gotta go now", Delores said without any further explanation of the event, "call me if you want to see me again, you guys have lot to discuss" ".Oh Stan, I'm so happy that she left, this whole thing is really freakin' me out now. What are we supposed to do next? Do you really think that there was a murder here? It sure looks like something happened don't you? I mean hey, the police use psychics to solve cases and she seems to know a lot and that "writing" you just did, whoa, that's scary!" "Ok. Jude, look since we've gone this far, let's go get the OUIJA Board and find out what it has to say! As we played with the board, we asked it question after question and it confirmed it all. You know Stan, now I know why this house was sitting here vacant so long and the bank forclosed on it. That guy Joel probably stole some mafia money. I think his girlfriend knew too much and he killed her. Do you think I'm just making this all up or what? Is that why these spirits are messing around with us here?" "Hey Jude, I'm Jewish remember, we don't believe in this psychic stuff. But something happened, that's for sure. Maybe it is her spirit that's trying to tell us about it.

Oh, I was so happy it was Friday. Stan went to pick up the boys. I wanted to forget everything and just have some fun with the kids. We spent the whole next day biking and walking in the woods near a small pond along with our dog Shabam. She was a lot easier to be with than Rufus so he was left in the house. We kept tossing sticks in the pond to watch Shabam dive in to get them. She was the funniest sight to see.....she could hardly swim at all and paddled vertically with just her head and front feet moving frantically just above the water. Arriving home we packed up Steve and Elliot for Stan to drive back to their mother's house. It was Saturday night and we had plans to go out dancing later in the evening. Kurt's voice yelled to me from downstairs. "Mom, ...Holly and I are going out for a bike ride...we're going over to Gary's house,...Ok."? ""All right just be careful, I want you both back within an hour. and watch out for your sister"! As I watched them ride down the street from my bedroom window and I had the house finally all to myself, I decided to take a nice long shower. I was about to turn on the shower but stopped and felt moved to go back and look out the window again. A lady drove up and jumped out carrying a child and I saw Kurt running after her with the bikes. I threw on some clothes and ran downstairs. "OH MY GOD!...HOLLY...WHAT HAPPENED"? The lady looked at me with a look of amazement. "Mam, you have a brave son here....your daughter fell off her bike headfirst over the handlebars and was lying in the street. Your son quickly picked her up and carried her to the side of the road. It was on a curve and I could have run over her! You better call an ambulance". I did that immediately and left a message at Joyce's house for Stan, hoping he'd get it before leaving his boys there. As soon as the rescue truck arrived we were taken to the emergency room where they stitched her up temporarily until the following day. Holly had broken her jaw. As the nurse was asking what happened, Kurt started rattling as many facts as he could about the accident. "Mom, I was so afraid after she fell off the bike that a car would hit her so I carried her to the side. I learned in Boy Scouts how to apply pressure to stop the bleeding so I kept my hand there and then that lady stopped and helped me. Mom is Holly going to be all right"? "Yes Kurt, I believe you just saved your sister's life....that sure deserves another Boy Scout Badge"! I tried to make the situation a little lighter so he wouldn't be so frightened. It was April 1st...but this was no joke!! Passing by her bedroom that night I heard her talking to someone quietly. "Holly, who are you talking to"? "Mom, I'm talking to a lady, she keeps telling me it's not going to hurt and I don't have any pain". "Holly, what lady are you talking about"? "Mom...the lady that comes to visit me". "Ok. Holly, but turn the lights out and get some sleep". I thought she was talking to an angel or something.....anyway, that's what I wanted to believe. The next six weeks were rough as Holly had to have her jaws wired shut with only space for a straw for liquid food.

(Stan)

"Honey, can we get out of here for a while? Let's go down to the Harborside for a drink. Maybe all these 'spirits' will just go away". "Good Idea Jude let's go! Ya know Jude, all that "witchy" psychic stuff yesterday really got to me, but I swear, my arm wrote by itself and it wasn't me writing I can tell that for sure! Eecchh, blood stains in the barn, the words "murder", Joel and those mafia guys last year....I dunno; I think we're letting our imaginations run wild"! "Sure Stan, how about the bells, how 'bout music downstairs in the night, how 'bout phones floating in the air, and by the way...Kurt told me that he saw Red Eyes looking at him in the barn last week". "ENOUGH HON, Ok., Ok.....I'm gettin' the chills, I got it,....we'd better get back to business. It's a good thing we rented this office away from the house ya know, away from all that "stuff" and the kids, and the dogs. Hey Jude, remember how we got that big "Spencer Gift" account from the New York Giftware Show we were in?" "Yeah Stan, the buyer called us...I should say she called me 'cause I was the one she talked to there. It was early in the morning a few days later after we got home and there I was....or should I say there we were.....sitting in the bed without a stitch of clothing on pretending to be in our office. You could hardly hold yourself from laughing as I took the order for our first huge account. Hmmmm, Jude I sure do remember, but it was hard to concentrate on the order or you!! **STAN!**....get serious...they weren't supposed to re-order until every three months but our jewelry has sold so well through their catalog that they're ordering every month. We just don't have the funds or the time necessary to get the merchandise made and shipped in time from Mexico, and Spencer Gifts doesn't pay us every 30days either....so now what?" "Well, I told you that the quality of our jewelry and our original designs would sell good....but I never thought it would sell this good...this fast....we may have to turn the account over to a bigger company than ours, maybe we can make a deal and still make a percentage of the profits, I'll look into it". "**WHAT..SELL THE BUSINESS...ARE YOU NUTS?**" "NO....I'm not nuts, you just don't know what business is all about yet!" "Are you calling me stupid?" "Did I say that? I said you just have a lot to learn!" "I HAVE A LOT TO LEARN? Listen my little Jew boy; **YOU** have a lot to learn. I know as much about this business as you do!" "You do, do you?....hey I've been in business for a lot of years,...where you been babe?" " Oh yeah? and you lost the friggin business and most of your bucks too! I'm 'outa here!" "Who do you think you're talkin' too; I'm the one who's been teachin' you and takin' care of your kids too!" SLAM! The door shut hard as I took off for nowhere in my little car after an argument. I could not stand confrontation, especially not from Stan.

(Judy)

What a jerk, if he thinks he's such a hot shot in business then why did he loose it? I'm glad we came to the office in two cars so I don't have to hang around and get more aggravated than I am. Man, I love my little Fiat sports car, it's the only place I feel peaceful. I'm so glad I took that mechanic's course and learned how to work on the alternator and change my brakes; I just wish it would stop falling apart. Boy, the Italians designed a great looking car, but that's about it with this one. I started to giggle as I remembered the time that I changed the brakes. I was so proud. I drove it home after spending all day on it and Stan drove the babysitter home in it. On the way back the muffler fell off so as he drove fast into the long driveway he let it roll to a stop so I wouldn't hear it and he waited until the next morning to tell me. But it's yellow, and its mine and I still love it! I drove everywhere until I cooled off from our little fight at the office but it was getting late and Kurt and Holly would be wondering where I was. As I pulled in the driveway, I saw a car to my left with it's headlights on teetering on top of the granite wall that stood about five feet from the ground. The wall separated the different heights of the land at that point and was very close to the road in the front of the house. OH NO!, Not again!. I knew the people in the car had already gone to the front door and would be really confused as to what had happened. They were just a few of the folks who had experienced the same thing, and the granite wall was starting to show the effects. Each granite block probably weighed several hundred pounds and one of them was pushed right out and down on top of the land below. As I entered the house the woman was crying and her husband kept repeating "I don't know what happened, I just don't know... I was driving slowly around the curve and I saw this woman standing right in the middle of it. It looked like she was in a rainstorm. I swerved to avoid her and that's when I hit the wall. My wife and I turned around to see if she was still there but she was nowhere in sight!" Stan and I just looked at each other. We had heard the same story quite a few times. Who is this mystery woman anyway? "Well look folks, at least you weren't hurt; would you like a cup of coffee or anything while Stan calls the tow truck for you?" "No we'll just wait outside for it but thank you so much for the offer". Stan and I always feel so bad for these people. It's always the same story. I wondered whether it was really the spirit of Sara appearing, the woman who was supposed to have been killed maybe by Joel but I was afraid to voice it. As I sat by our window and watched the couple sitting on the wall near the car I couldn't help thinking again about all the strange things that have been going on since we moved in. Ken and Lin stayed over one night and woke up with a dream of someone in a coffin. Another friend who had slept here had the same dream. Linda always felt that someone was in back of her. Music where there is no music, doors opening and closing with no one there, phones floating in the air, mafia showing up at our door, items disappearing, bells in the barn....WHAT NEXT? As I looked over my shoulder to the back of the living room I saw that stupid red eyed troll staring at me that we bought at that strange Flaming Cauldron Store. It always freaked me out. Oh good, the tow truck arrived.

"Mom", Kurt asked, "why do people keep hitting our wall,. Are they driving too fast?" I didn't want to scare him with what I thought, so I just agreed. "Yes, they probably do and that's why I don't want you, Holly or Stevie and Elliot playing anywhere near the front of the house or that wall. There's plenty of property all around here and in the back for all of you to play on. and I especially don't want any of you to cross the road near the pond." "Mom, I'm afraid of that man who lives on the other side of the pond up on the hill, every time I see anyone walking near the pond he comes out of his house with a big rifle. He even shot it in the air once". "I know honey, I've already reported him to the police but they don't seem to be in any hurry to check into it, that's why I insist that you stay in the back of our house for now, Ok.?" "Sure mom, hey, after dinner, can we all play with the OUIJA Board? Maybe it can tell us why everyone keeps hitting the wall". Kurt was always curious like a detective but I didn't want him to find out about Sara. "Hey, I have a better idea; let's see what the board says about a buried treasure on the property. I think those mafia guys were looking for something!" "YEHHH"... the kids were really into that! As we all sat around the OUIJA Board, our excitement level grew as it spelled out the numbers **3 8 0 0 0**, then the words **BURIED** and finally **YARD !** "Did you see that?" Stan said with a look of excitement in his eyes that I hadn't seen lately. "That guy Joel must have buried some stolen mafia cash somewhere on the property and you know what?...$38,000's a lot of cash....finders keepers right? I think we should get one of those metal detectors, maybe it can locate the box the cash is in". Stan, take it easy, we just can't start digging up Arnie's yard without telling him....I mean it's in the back and in full view of his house and front door!" "Yeah, you're right babe" Stan replied with a slight look of disappointment in his face. STAN..c'mon, you would really do that without telling Arnie?, that's stealing!" "Oh Jude you are such a goody-two-shoes, get off the soap box will ya, I still think this is all a big joke but it would be fun to poke around anyway...who knows what we might find? I'll go and tell Arnie and see what he has to say O.K.? Look, we've already told him about Joel, he actually heard some stories about the guy too and he knows about the strange stuff that's been happening around here. By the way, where DOES he get all his money from anyway? He drives a Corvette and owns a sailboat....he sure lives good. He says he's in construction but he never gives me any real details. I've even wondered whether he's connected with the mafia too. Ya know the bank that owns this property is connected to some pretty suspicious looking characters. I've met a few of them and they all look like mafia types and the property was sold to Arnie without ever being shown to anyone else. Oh well, whatever, I'll talk to him tomorrow.

Arnie and his girlfriend Janet got real excited over what the OUIJA Board said and he even had a metal detector handy so off we all went on the treasure hunt. The kids were running around with small shovels as we dug each hole. The back of our house looked like giant gophers had burrowed into it everywhere. "Hey look", Arnie shouted, "the metal detector has found something". Arnie and Stan dug furiously and only a few feet down hit a metal box. The air was full of anticipation as the small tin box was opened. To everyone's disappointment the little box was empty and anyway it was much too small to have held any large amounts of money. The metal detector located other places but in each hole there was only an old can and not much more. "STAN", Arnie yelled, "YA think it might be hidden in the well?" Directly in back of the small rear cement slab was an old well which had a large cement cover over it that none of us, including the kids ever bothered with.

"Hey Arnie", Stan answered back with a smirk, ""You want to go down there? Go for it friend, there's probably snakes and who knows what else!" "Yeah Stan, you may be right, forget it, not me,...let's cover up these holes and call it a day". The possibility of hitting it rich was over but it was kind of fun especially for the kids and us, so it wasn't a complete loss. The following weeks were filled with periods of more digging and more nothing of anything valuable being found. Arnie even joined in from time to time. One of those times he took us aside with some information that really shook us up. "Hey you guys", he said sadly, "Ummmm, I need to tell you that I've decided to sell the property but I'll give you the right of first refusal to buy it". Our expressions went blank as we tried to process what he had just told us. "You're kidding? Right Arnie?" Stan said in disbelief. "No, actually I have to sell it 'cause I need the cash to finance a lot of other construction I'm involved in, but hey look, you could buy the house for $75,000 and at least stay here but the barn, my house and the carriage house is a separate package. Let me know what you think, there's no rush". Stan and I walked back into the house in silence and Stan finally opened up and said "you know hon, there's nothing more I'd like in this world than to own this property but now it's $10,000 more than I could have bought it for three years ago and it doesn't even include the barn and the other buildings and land. Besides that Judy, it really needs tons of repairs. I dunno, this is definitely NOT good news, we just may have to wind up moving". MOVING? my heart sank as I heard Stan speak that word. "You're joking right?", I responded sadly, "I love it here even with all the 'spirit stuff' going on and besides, suppose we never find out what happened to Joel's girlfriend Sara?" I don't know about all that, gorgeous, all I know is that we'd better start preparing ourselves for the possibility that Arnie could sell this place sooner than we think. It's a very desirable area and a historically valuable piece of property. It won't last long on the market". One by one the buyers came looking. At first we made sure that the place looked clean. "Hey Stan, are we crazy...let's make it look sloppy....pour some water on the floor and in the basement and make it look like water leaks....throw some dog food around and some mouse traps too. Maybe we can scare away any buyers!" I said it half jokingly, but we decided to do it anyway.

EXILED

(Judy)

My heart sank at the thought of moving from my beautiful dream home. I felt my whole world caving in. I knew that potential buyers were coming over in the afternoon so I got the children together quickly from outside. "Kids, help me with a project O.K.? Let's put some water on the floor in the basement and on one of the ceilings to make it look like we have water leaks in the house". They got all excited about that and I then proceeded to spray water all over one section of the ceiling in the kitchen. I wanted it to be very obvious and it looked like normal water damage when I got through. Arnie brought in the buyers at about 2 pm. They looked around the house in each room and every area of it. I thought they'd never leave. They looked at the ceiling and questioned Arnie. "I'll look into it" he answered them as he turned and gave me a dirty look. "Arnie I noticed that there is also some water in the basement area" the prospective lady buyer said with some concern. By this time Arnie was really getting pissed off. He knew my game but I didn't care. "Well that's just a small problem", she said to her husband. "I love everything about this place, it needs a lot of work but I still love it". I was screaming inside. I wanted Stan to buy it but I knew it was impossible. They finally left about 45 minutes later after walking all over the outside of the property. As soon as they left, I felt every fear and disappointment bubbling out of me. "Mom don't cry", Kurt said, "it will be O.K.". Kurt was so loving. Holly didn't understand the whole situation but hated to see me cry as well. "I'm sorry kids but we may have to move. That couple that just left may buy the property". "Mommy let's buy it first". Holly, we don't have enough money to buy it honey. "I have some money in my piggy bank and some money grampa gave me, will that help?" "Thanks kids but it takes a lot of money." "I don't want to move Mom", Kurt said sadly. "Me either" Holly added. "I know how you both feel and I don't want to move out of our home either. I know it's spooky sometimes but it's been ours for three years." Just then Stan pulled up and when he walked in the kitchen he knew something wasn't right. "What's going on Jude? Why is the ceiling so wet and the house so messy!" I chuckled, "I did what you said and made the house look undesirable but the man and wife that just left still loved it. STAN...THEY MAY BUY IT!" I felt Stan's heart sink.

Arnie didn't waste any time. He came over immediately with the bad news. "She wants to buy the house" he said with a big smile. "But look you guys, I still want to give you first bids on it, isn't there anyway you can buy it?" Stan just stared at Arnie with a sinking feeling. "Yeah Arnie, we'd sure like to stay here but our finances can't handle the burden". "I'm sorry Stan, I know you all love this place but if she gets approved she wants to move in right away". "Arnie!" Stan said with slight choking in his voice, "We need time to find another house and time to move too!" "Relax guys, I'm not making you move tomorrow, you'll have plenty of time, don't worry". When Arnie left, we sat down and stared at each other. The kids had gone upstairs and I was real happy they didn't hear the whole conversation. "Well babe, we'd better start looking for a place to live huh? I'm so sorry that I can't buy this place for you, I know how much you and all the kids love it." I tried to control the tears rolling down my cheeks. As I looked at Stan with his head hanging down looking at the floor, I tried to console him. "Honey you have given us three wonderful years here. If it weren't for you, I'd still be living in my 3rd floor apartment. And thanks to you it has brought our families closer. We've had so many great memories together...don't worry, we'll find another place and create new memories, and hey! we'll leave all the ghosts from the past here Ok?" Stan laughed a little but he knew my heart was breaking as I spoke. It didn't take much longer to get the news that the house had actually been bought and that we had to move. I was happy that it was July and that the children were out of school. We searched everywhere in the area but found nothing for rent. "Oh Stan, I love this area but there just isn't anything much to rent around here and what there is we can't afford and we only have a month to move!" "Something will come up Jude" Stan said reassuringly. I knew we needed a house not an apartment, and a landlord that would accept two children and not mind two other boys visiting on weekends, much less our two large dogs and two cats, some fish and parents who weren't married but just living together. Of course in the 1970's that was the thing to do. In my mind though, one failed marriage was enough!

Stan pulled up in the driveway with excitement all over him. "JUDE, I think I found us a place. It's not close to here, its two towns over but it's real cute four bedrooms, country style with lots of land around it! Ken and Linda know this man from their town and he mentioned he was looking for a renter. I contacted him and went to see the property. It's not as big as our house but I think you'll like it. The owner said we can paint the walls if we want to and I'll have to buy some large area carpeting. You know what hon; I'm going to look around for some new furniture too!" My heart was still aching over the whole move but I knew we had no choice, Stan seemed so excited so I tried to look happy too. "There's only one problem babe, you have to say that we're married. This couple is very religious and won't rent to anyone living together". "Well screw that, that's his problem, I'm not getting married just so we can live there!" "Calm down Jude, you and this "marriage" thing. I said 'pretend we're married". "O.k., I can do that I suppose, but I still don't like lying, you know that!" We stopped at the owner's house and talked with them for a while and he drove us up to the house for rent which was quite a distance away from his house up a narrow one lane winding driveway. The house was located in the woods with lots of land around it and a separate garage. There was another home not too far away but neither that house, the owner's nor the street could be seen from there. The privacy was just what we needed. As we walked through the house, I got excited. The children's rooms were upstairs, one on one side, one on the other with a narrow hall between them. We had to bend our heads down a little to get into them but the kids had no trouble at all. Downstairs was a good sized master bedroom, a second bedroom, one full bath, a roomy kitchen, a dining area near it and a large living room with a screened in porch behind it. Stan was happy to see my excitement as we drove back to the owner's house to fill out the application papers. We had to wait a day or so because he had more people to interview but we were confident we would be the renters. I just hated putting "married" on the application. I don't like *deception* of any kind and I especially didn't like the idea of me being the deceiver! "Judy, Ken and Lin told me it's the only way we can rent it!" "I know Stan, don't worry I'll go along with the lie, but I still don't like it!" It didn't take a few days; the phone rang later that day with the good news. We were moving into our new home immediately. Desi went back to live with her mother Myra. I kind of missed her but it would have been too hard for her to leave high school in her senior year. We asked the landlord if we could show the house to our children including Stan's two boys and they didn't seem to mind. The kids were very excited they loved the property and the bedrooms and there was even a small tree house already built in the back of the house.

We began packing and started noticing that little things I would put down on a table began to disappear. As I gathered some of our things together, I found the children's baby books and sat and began to reminisce and realized how quickly they had grown. I kept the books from other books so I could pack them separately. "STAN....can you bring me some more boxes I need to pack up the pantry and some special albums I want to keep together". Hmmmm, here's Kurt's baby album but where's Holly's? I knew I put them down together. I asked Stan and the kids but no one had seen it anywhere. I know I had only left the room for two minutes and both albums were there....what's going on here? "Stan", I yelled, "why do things keep disappearing?" I sat down to get my head together, nothing was making any sense. "Judy, maybe it's a good thing we're getting out of here, there's just too much unexplained stuff happening". "Well, I can't say I'm happy about that but I'll still miss my house. "S T A N N N !!" "Yeah hon, what's the matter?" Okay, that does it, I'm ticked! Kurt's baby album is now missing too. This ghost or whatever is trying to play games with my head. You saw the books Stan; you know I'm not crazy!" We looked everywhere but never found them. We also started to find little puddles of water in the middle of the kitchen floor. I'd wipe them up and they'd appear again later on. Sadness saturated the air as we all packed and counted the days to depart.

Finally, moving day arrived and I was so glad that my kids were with their dad. I wanted them to keep the good memories and not have to struggle with leaving. We hired a moving van that had enough room in it to pick up two fairly new couches we had purchased from a private party. "Hey Stan, we're all done with all of this, let's go down to Smitty's Bar and Grill tonight and get together with our friends and have some laughs, we sure could use some of that"! "Hey, love to Jude, this whole thing has been very emotional and draining,.let's go!" The night was great but we decided to get home early as we still had a lot to do the next day. As we pulled around the curve to our house, we could see the whole area lit up, but then just as quickly, we saw the light go off from our house. Was someone in it I thought? Maybe Janet, she and Arnie had a key that must be it. There were still some lights on in the sunroom but as we pulled into the back of the house, they went off too. We entered the house with caution, not knowing if Janet or someone was in there but found no one. Our dog Shabam was really happy to see us and followed us from room to room. She loved everyone except any person who looked like they might harm us or our kids. She could get real aggressive if that happened. We both jumped as we heard pounding on the back door. Who could it be at this hour? As Stan opened the door, there stood Janet with a real funny upset look on her face. "THANKS A LOT YOU GUYS!" she blurted out, half laughing, half mad. "FOR WHAT" we answered, with not a clue as to what she was saying. "**FOR WHAT**?. She said loudly, "for not inviting me to your party tonight, that's FOR WHAT!" "Uhhh, Janet. We were down at Smitty's tonight, ask Arnie, he was there with us,...we didn't have any party here...what are you talking about?" "C'mon, you can't kid me, I saw lots of people in the house, loud music, and lights were going on and off... it looked like a disco night club". We both looked at each other in bewilderment. We saw lights on when we came home but then they all quickly went out. "YOU know, there was a really bright light from Kurt's bedroom that was on all night, couldn't miss that!" Janet said loudly. We took her upstairs and showed her that Kurt's room was completely empty; it didn't even have a ceiling light in it, just a floor lamp we had packed up downstairs. "O.k., now you are scaring me, then who was here?" "Uhhhhh....hate to tell you but it had to be all the mysterious spirits in the house, there's no other explanation; really Janet, didn't you just see us drive up? Like I said, ask Arnie, he was with us all night at Smitty's". "BYE, I'm outa here", Janet yelled as she bolted across the lawn back to her house.

"Okay Jude, still want to stay here tonight?" "Sure Stan, what the hell, we have to get some sleep for the move". We opened the couch which was still in the sunroom and crawled in. I had to go to the bathroom though and as I walked up the stairs, I heard funny noises but when you gotta go you gotta go. The house was pretty dim with only a few small lights on here and there. All of a sudden I heard a loud voice groaning. Shabam and the cat freaked out and all three of us went scampering down the stairs as fast as we could. I jumped into the bed under the covers with Stan and the cat joined us on top. Stan and I grabbed each other and began to make love. All of a sudden it felt like a very heavy man with a big belly and a rough beard was on top of me. I began to get scared and thought it was just my imagination. Stan is a very gentle guy but this was very uncomfortable. This person, whoever it was, who was on top of me was treating me very rough and hurting me. I yelled "**STOP!**, WHAT'S HAPPENING?" I pushed Stan aside and he yelled "WHAT WAS THAT? You were different, like a mannequin and I felt like a heavy man with a rough beard". "STAN, that's how it felt,....Oh my God Stan can spirits make love through people? I want out of here!" "Sleep tight hon, we'll be outa here before you know it". There was a slight wind outside the many windowed sunroom. We never had any shades or curtains hung over any of the downstairs windows as the house was located far away from the road. No one could really see in but we could see anyone approaching. The wind blew some large bushy branches across the side of the room and it made a very eerie sound which only added to the 'spooky' time we spent that night. One of our cats slept soundly on top of our covers and our dog Shabam on the floor nearby. Rufus, our oversized sheepdog, had never budged from his sleeping area. We loved him but he always seemed to be in a fog and he was a lot of work to keep clean and brushed. At over 80 pounds he was after all a purebred Sheepdog with papers a mile long and, like Shabam, had become one of the family.

The moving van came early, and as weary looking as we were, we decided to shower and freshen up in our new home. Besides, we still had to stop at the house where we had purchased the new couches before arriving at our new residence. So, after a quick bite of cereal and a cup of coffee we managed to make, we stood on the lawn and looked lovingly at the home we started our lives together. "Whad'ya think my Jude? It doesn't seem possible does it? Three years gone by already, well.....you're right, the memories were well worth it". I heard Stan talking, but my mind was anywhere but on the moment. The word "memories" did register though, and that's where my thoughts would always be when thinking about all the days we spent living at this address. There could never be anything quite like it again. This I knew for sure in my heart.

(Stan)

The shock of moving out of our dream house passed, and we all settled into our new cottage in the woods. Ken and Lin, who had become much closer friends and business associates, helped us move in and paint the dining and living room areas. They loved to disco like we did and smoked grass and drank mostly wine on occasion with us. Ken was very astute as far as the combined jewelry businesses we both shared. We had already participated in some local giftware shows in malls and flee markets and developed some really good displays and sales abilities.

"Hey Domingo", Ken yelled over the phone, often calling me by the name given to me by our Mexican Jewelry guide Serafin in Taxco, Mexico. "Si Senor", I answered, "what's up friend?" Ken and I had become almost as close as brothers. He was a perfect addition to my partner Denny who had moved to San Diego with Jackie the year before. Ken and Denny didn't have much time to get to know each other before Den left town and I had felt real deserted at the time. I know of a really terrific event called the "Spring Fest Expo" that we can get into. It's happening within a month in our neighbor state but we have to submit the application and fees right away and we also have to construct some kind of booth to display our wares, what do you think? I think we could make a fortune there, almost a million people pass through the gates, and it's on for one full week!" Ken sounded really excited and I got excited too after thinking about the possibilities of it. "Yeah Mr. Marketeer Man, it sounds like a win, win to me...great, let's meet up tomorrow and plan it all out O.K?" We put together plans for a booth with a straw thatched half roof to look like a Mexican hut. Thank God for Ken's dad who knew a lot more about carpentry or we could not have constructed the whole thing by ourselves. In fact, our patience with each other reached some pretty strained levels during the process, but, it was finally finished and off we went. I had purchased a small older van, looked like a red-cross van with its red and white colors. The booth and all of other equipment barely fit into it and the front right side of the windshield cracked some when we slammed the back door shut shoving one of the support poles into it. Ken had also borrowed his uncle's RV for all of us to sleep in while we were there. All in all it turned out to be a pretty memorable time and we didn't do too bad financially, but it was very exhausting work as we had to be up and running by 8am and the crowds didn't go home until 8pm.

Returning back home everything remained on the quiet side. The kids had pretty well adjusted to life in their new home. Though it never really bothered us, some of our friends didn't like driving up the long dark driveway at night; said it felt like "Freddy Krueger" would jump out at them especially from the small Christmas tree farm directly in front of the house. Judy, however, had suddenly become not only house bound but literally had a rough time even leaving the bedroom and she couldn't explain why. We eventually chalked it up to maybe a depression over leaving the old house as the cause, although she felt it was different than that. In any case, I managed to get her out enough to get over it. It was the fall of 1978 and Disco was still in full swing. Ken and Lin still went out dancing with us as much as we could, especially to an area that had an old converted mansion. Some people drove up in restored 1930's vehicles and even wore period clothing. The spinning disco ball and the unending music was all we really ever wanted to do together as couples. For most of the rest of the year it seemed as though we were free of the 'spirit' stuff from our former residence and we were not doing too bad either financially with our jewelry sales. One of the smaller discothèques in town that we would frequent with Ken and Lin turned out to be a perfect place to hold a reception for my son Steve's Bar Mitzvah, a Jewish ceremony that was the change for a boy to become a man and enter the community as a responsible adult. "Judy, how does Disco-Mitzvah sound"? "Disco-Mitzvah? "Stan, that's so clever...what a fun idea, man, your family will love that....the young people will really love it and that's really who it's for..right"?

We always tried to cut our expenses when going out with Ken and Lin. Judy or Lin would sneak a small bottle of wine in their large purse so that we could keep re-filling our original glasses first ordered. Judy was still on my case about it and she was never happy with sneaking or lying and Lin wasn't too comfortable with the idea either but Ken and I always won out with our "rationalization" of saving money. The Bar Mitzvah day was arriving soon and I was getting very nervous to be around all of the friends of my ex wife's and mine and also of all my family members who I hadn't seen since my divorce. I had left my Jewish surroundings and had fallen in love with and moved in with a "Shicksa" a negative description for a non-Jewish girl. We had invited a lot of our friends to the occasion, none of them Jewish of course, so the tension for me was maxed out that day. "Stan", it was my ex-wife on the phone. "I understand that a lot of your friends are coming to the Bar Mitzvah, could you please tell them to dress conservatively....you know....the Temple is very conservative and so are a lot of the family and our old friends". "O.K, sure Joyce, I'll let Judy know so she can relate that information". **"JUDY",** I yelled half laughing at the same time I got off the phone. "You'll never guess what Joyce wants us to do!" "What now, Stan?" "Oh nothing serious,...really funny when you think of it, she wants us to tell all of our friends to dress conservatively for the Bar Mitzvah. She knows we all like to dress up really wild at discos and she knows that we like to drink and smoke a lot too. Does she not get it that this is a DISCO-Mitzvah Reception!" "Oh, she said that did she?" Judy didn't waste any time phoning our friends. "Hi Lin, listen, do me a favor will you, dress up in the most flashy outfit you have for the Bar Mitzvah, and that goes for Ken too...O.K.?" (Judy phoned each and every friend on the list and gave them the same pitch).

Before leaving the house, I lit up the first of a few joints of marijuana I had and also had a half glass of wine. Judy was always the happy smiley fun person and didn't need anything like that. She gave me a few funny looks as we drove off but she understood my anxieties and let it go. Judy was wearing a strapless jumpsuit underneath her full length leather coat as we sat patiently for the service to begin at the Temple. One of my uncles came up close to congratulate us and as he did, he looked at Judy and said... "Can't wait to see what you have on under that coat!". Did he say what I thought I just heard? Suddenly, my name was called as the father of the Bar Mitzvah boy to come up on stage to the pulpit and take a seat next to the Rabbi. I was somewhat 'zoned out' but managed to look sober. The Rabbi leaned over to me and whispered "you're number 7". (number 7 ?...I thought to myself...what's he talking about?) Oh yeah, I'm the seventh person to get up and recite one of the Hebrew prayers that morning in honor of my son. I did it somehow and no one really knew what was going on inside me...although at the moment the Rabbi asked that question, it nearly freaked me out! The reception went great and my ex-wife quickly realized that absolutely none of our friends were dressed as she had hoped. In fact, they were all dressed appropriately for the disco sounds which were being blasted on a hundred thousand dollar sound system. At one point she signaled me to tone it down, I looked over at the DJ and put my thumb UP....making it even louder. But all of the crowd, especially the older folks, loved it 'cause it included some of the ethnic Jewish songs I had planned like "The Hora", a Jewish celebration dance and "Ba Mer Bis Du Shane" an old Yiddish song meaning "by me you are beautiful". Comments from everyone were simply that it was the best Bar Mitzvah reception they had ever attended.

"Stan its Ken on the phone". "Hi Ken what's up?" "Hey buddy; the Bar Mitzvah was really terrific...what fun having all of our friends together in one place." "Yeah Ken, I only made one bad mistake". "What's that Stan, didn't look like anything was out of place!" "Uh,..not that way; I instructed the Disco to have an open bar and everyone took advantage of it.....uhh...I didn't have the additional funds to pay for it yesterday,....sooooo I had to ask my ex-wife to kick in her share,...and she was NOT a happy camper". "Whoops, better you than me buddy. Listen,....there's another giftware show we should go to , its in New York City and we have to apply today or we won't be able to get in...its the yearly Christmas show..we could do really good there". "New York City.....The Big Apple!!...yeah...in a heartbeat Ken, I don't even have to ask Jude about that; do it and let me know what I owe you". Within a week after Thanksgiving we all found ourselves at the New York Show. "Would you believe what's going on here" I said shocked by what I saw. "There are people walking around the show passing out free samples of marijuana, and look at that booth...they're selling "edible panties" for women!" "Hey folks, love your jewelry", our fascination with the activity around us was interrupted by the female voice in the aisle. "Well hi there, glad you like it; I'm Stan, this is Judy and these are our friends Ken and Lin". "My name is Max, short for Maxine...I hate that name. I really like your jewelry but I have to leave now, could we meet later at my apartment, you know, after the show ends this afternoon?" We all looked at each other and agreed, "give us the address; we'll get over there somehow". We hadn't even checked into a hotel so it sounded like a plan to us....but then, almost anything new and fun sounded like a plan to all of us. Max was about our age, in her late 30's, with stylish clothes and more than very interesting to talk to. She had this strange "aura" about her. As we found out later, she was what was called a 'Claire Voyant' She bought some of our jewelry and some of Ken's but we became more interested in what she had to say than us selling anything to her. We actually ordered some food in and wound up staying overnight with her. Strangely enough, she felt more like a long lost friend we hadn't seen in a long time. "Stan", Judy said with some reservation in her tone, "I like Max, but don't you feel a little uncomfortable around her,....I mean with all that Claire Voyant talk and all?" "Yeah, a little, but hey hon we talked about our old house a lot and about when Linda's dad was located by the Ouija Board, maybe she can shed some more light on what was going on with all that..ya think?" "I'd almost prefer not to know babe but anyway she said she'd like to visit us when she gets a chance, we'll see! By the way Stan I didn't want to say anything before we left home but some small puddles of water are showing up again in our new home." "Listen hon, this New York Show and Max did me in; can we get out of here early? I'm not feeling good about any of this; we didn't really sell much anyway".

> *"Why was I still feeling this 'ominous cloud' around me?*
> *There was a heaviness I couldn't explain to anyone!"*

"Hey Jude?" "What my wealthy husband?" Judy was always lifting me up and encouraging me with her words although I couldn't always say I believed her. Now that we were in this remote old cottage house in a 2nd rate town which really wasn't nearly up to the high standards of where we used to live, I had started to feel like the biggest failure ever. "You know, it looks like retail and wholesale jewelry buyers have changed over to gold. Silver just doesn't seem to be selling very good anymore. Remember what I said about selling off the Spencer Gift account? I think it would be a good idea to find a buyer pretty soon!" "I'll tell you what sweetheart it's a good thing I got that Jewelry Designer retainer account a few months ago, at least it's paying a steady weekly salary! I really enjoy the job and it sure is keeping my spirits up". "Oh yeah, I'm certainly thankful for that too Stan....but I'm not convinced that we should sell off the Spencer account yet, after all its steady catalog business, silver or not, maybe we can still find a way to fill the orders!" "Well, we'll see. I'm still a little nervous though even about the retainer account we have". "How come Stan, they really like you and all the designs you've come up with right?" "Yeah but they've just hired on some real dorky looking' bow tied know it all midget who's going to take over their merchandising program. He and I don't really see eye to eye but I've been trying to appease him and make him happy...and you know what? I can almost not believe where he lives!" "Where he lives, what do mean hon?" "Judith! The company is located over 30 miles away from here in the next state. He and his wife are friends of the people who just bought our old house. They just built their new house on the lot just next to it!" "WHAT?....Boy, this is either coincidence or more trouble following us Stan, I don't think I want to go through any more "funny stuff" again!'

(Judy)

Stan didn't show it as much but I really missed our old house. I loved the area, knew tons of people in the town and now I feel like part of me is missing. I hated it especially when the kids were in school and Stan was away at his design consultant job. That would leave me all alone almost the entire day. Somehow, I could handle what was going on in the other house but this one was too remote and felt spooky. When it was getting to late afternoon, the house was in total blackness all around it. We still had our office at least and I could escape sometimes to fill our jewelry orders, but I noticed that the jewelry orders had grown faster than what we could supply due mostly to the huge Spencer Gift Catalog sales. They were now ordering every month instead of three times a year as stated in our original contract. Hearing the phone ringing and after fumbling with my keys, I finally entered the office and was barely able to answer it after just about leaping to get it. It was the buyer from Spencer Gifts. After I hung up I sat back in my chair and let out a big sigh. It was another huge order. Most people would be jumping all over with joy after receiving an order like that, but it wasn't even the money that was necessary to supply it, all of our items were hand made in Mexico and had to be shipped to us directly before we could mail it out to our customers. Spencer Gifts did not always pay monthly so it was putting a real strain on us financially. As I sat pondering over our situation, Stan walked in. "Hi honey, what are you doing here so early?" He knew by my expression that I knew something was definitely wrong. "Lost my job! Remember I told you about the new guy they hired and I felt very uncomfortable around,....well...he let me go! Judy, I was just a design consultant. I got along with everyone and they were all happy with my designs but this guy wanted me to join in the company's daily meetings every morning but when I told him we had to drive to Florida to see your dad next week he then said go but don't come back. I explained that I could work on the road and overnight him the designs but this guy has been a pain in the ass since the day the company hired him. I think he just wants his nephew to have my job. Ya know, I knew in my 'gut' that something like this might happen when I found out he just built his new home within earshot of our old house. On top of that, you know, the people who bought our house are friends of his. The whole situation smelled rotten." I didn't know what to say to Stan, he worked so hard at everything, (at least when he wasn't smokin' weed) and I didn't realize how much all the losses had affected him since we first met. Now, we also didn't have the funds to put into our business, keep the office running or to get out of our contract with Spencer. Stan and I were getting very discouraged at just about everything. The giftware shows weren't even pulling in the sales they used to 'cause by now people were beginning to switch over to gold. Mama and Poppa stores weren't ordering like before and on top of that, Spencer Gifts were putting us into a financial bind.

"Jude, I've been doing a lot of thinking about this business. Ya know, we definitely have to give up the office and I really think it's time we also gave up this business as well!" "WHAT?....first our house, then your retainer account and now our business! C'mon Stan, we've worked so hard to build it all!" "Hon, I'm at a loss. I don't know what to say or what else to do. I've done some research and found a company in Pennsylvania that's willing to take the Spencer account off our hands but we'd also have to give him the names of our suppliers in Mexico. Look, he has a lot of bucks and can handle it and he'll buy our entire inventory too!" We just sat there depressed and bewildered. Neither of us had any words left. "Ok. Stan, just do it!" I said, hardly able to mumble or even believe the words coming out of my mouth. It wasn't long before we found ourselves driving to Pennsylvania and receiving a check for our entire jewelry inventory As we drove home, I started to think more clearly about how we had handled the situation. "Stan? Did we just sell him the jewelry and Spencer Gift contract but not all of our other accounts? Are we crazy?" "Judy, I grabbed the first person that showed an interest, otherwise we could have been sued by Spencer". "But Stan, that's not what our contract was for". "I know babe but I can't get into any legal hassles anymore, I'm tired of it all".

With not much left over in sales coming in or cash we had from the sale of our inventory, I decided to take a Real Estate Course, jumped in the middle of the class and caught up by studying day and night. I just squeezed by to take the test and passed. I was so proud of myself. During the test Stan had gone to a nearby McDonald's to wait for my results. When the testing was over, I ran over to meet him and he greeted me with a big smile. "Honey, honey, I passed the test and I am already hooked up with a local realtor isn't that great?" "WOW Judy, I knew you could do it". I could see that Stan was bustin' at the bit to tell me something. "I have some unbelievable news for you also.....we just won $5,000. I ordered a muffin and some coffee and got a scratch off contest Three $5000 matched!" "Are you sure Stan", I asked not fully confident in what he was telling me. "Oh yeah, I went to the counter and if you are any kind of a winner they give you a special envelope to mail the award in. I ran to the Post Office to mail it. We rejoiced all day long thinking about all the things we'd be doing now that our future was a lot more secure. Well, it didn't last too long. Within two weeks we received a letter back stating..."Thank you for playing our contest, better luck next time". In it was a picture of a losing prize with Stan's forged signature. "STAN? What are they talking about" "Oh no Jude, I have a black and white copy but I didn't send it certified, I was too excited. Look, I'll bring it to the McDonald's manager". When we got there, the manager and the girl that gave Stan the envelope were no longer employed there. We argued and got really upset but the instructions called for a registered letter. Anyone could have hijacked the envelope and cashed in the prize.

What's wrong? Why is Stan being so deceived? Why did he do that? Why did he give up his real estate business and now our jewelry business? He just keeps giving everything he works hard for away? ***I feel defeat all around us****. No matter what we try, it falls apart!"*

We remained very upset for a long time. In all the excitement Stan just mailed it in never looking at the instructions and never expecting anyone to rob him. McDonald's wouldn't have given him the envelope unless the manager checked out the winning prize but you can't fight Corporate even with proof. Someone had hi-jacked the envelope and forged his name on a prize that he didn't submit. It wasn't even a good forgery at that. Our friends started looking at us strangely but we knew that our story was 'over the top' so we dropped it, but our hearts ached for quite a while. Fear began creeping into every aspect of my being. It seemed that no matter how hard we worked, the rug kept being pulled out from under us. Even in my real estate sales, accounts I landed were being snatched or stolen by other agents. I worked hard but I wasn't a fighter so I gave up. Real estate sales weren't for me. Stan tried everything to get work but times were hard. He even went to the Welfare Office and offered to cut lawns but he was told that he was not a 'minority' sorry!"

As I looked out the window in dismay one day, I saw Kurt lying on the ground. Kurt was a boy that never complained much even if he was sick. I ran out the door..."KURT! What's wrong honey?" "Mom, my side hurts really bad". I went to touch him and he screamed. We got him to the Emergency Room in time to find out that his appendix was about to burst. I was questioned about it from the doctor but Kurt had never let me know anything up 'till that day. Thank God it all turned out O.k. Kurt's dad had some insurance and Kurt healed real fast. My insides were still jumping from all of the turn of events and I couldn't help wondering what might be next. As the days passed, we began to notice many strange things happening in the house but there was one particular evening that shook us all up. As I was doing the dishes, I spotted headlights coming up the darkened dirt driveway very slowly. It had to be someone we knew because no one else but our friends and the landlord knew the house was back here. Holly ran to the window excited to see who it was. "Mommy, its Suzanne's car". Holly loved Suzanne. She was one of our most cheerful friends and she loved to visit Holly especially. She was a friend of Jackie and they had always worked together as hairdressers. We flicked on the front porch lights and went to the door to greet Suzanne, but her car kept rolling past to the rear of the house and turned around. Stan ran to the back of the house to see what she was doing and then back to the kitchen to join us. We waited for the car to stop but it kept on rolling slowly past; the tires making that funny crunching sound against the gravel driveway. We could kind of hear the motor silently rumbling and an image of Suzanne at the wheel. As the car vanished back down the dirt path, we noticed the license plate on it, "DESINE". For sure that was Suzanne alright, who could miss that gold colored Datson300 with that obvious license plate. Holly started to cry. "Mommy, why didn't she come in? Why is she leaving?" I couldn't answer her because something was very strange about the whole thing. We had all seen her car and we could kind of make out Suzanne driving it although her image was blurred by the inside of the dark car but there was no doubt about the car itself or the license plate. The car almost looked like it was floating by and Suzanne usually drove up really fast so nothing made any sense. "Holly" I said reassuringly, "let's call her and make sure that was really her". "Hi Holly", Suzanne's voice on the other end of the phone cheered up Holly's tears for a moment. "What's the matter honey?" "Suzanne,...did you or someone else borrow your car, come here and drive away? We ran to the door to see you and your car kept going down the driveway. If it was you, how come you didn't stop and come in?" "Ummmm....Holly, I'm still at work, I didn't come to your house!" Holly dropped the phone and really started to cry. "Suzanne? What did you say to Holly and why didn't you come in tonight?" "Judy, I swear, my car and I have been in the salon all night, are you sure it wasn't a car that looked like mine?" "No Suzi Q, it definitely had your "DESINE" license plate on it. Ok. Suzanne, no problem". "Hey wait a minute Judy", Suzanne replied, "You're freakin' me out and I haven't had anything to smoke or drink either". "I know Suzanne, I have no answers, I'll talk to you tomorrow. I have to go quiet Holly down but she'll be all right". Kurt made a funny joke about it but Stan and I knew that something was very strange about the whole thing. All this 'spirit' stuff was still around us and we couldn't seem to shake it no matter where we were or what we were doing. Fear can bring in deception and spiritual awakenings. We had opened the door to the dark side of the world just like a web and we didn't know how to get out.

(Stan)

"HI STAN", it was Max's voice from New York, the gal we had stayed with during the Holiday Giftware Show. "Hi Max, boy it's good to hear your voice. How've you been? We haven't talked to you in a few months". "Well Stan, is Judy home?" "No, I'm here alone; it's a cloudy, damp, drizzly day. I'm kind of down in the dumps; we've been going through some tough times since we saw you last". "I know, let's see, you're not in business anymore, weird spirit stuff hanging around right?" "RIGHT Max, how'd you know all that....oh yeah sure, I forgot...you're a Claire Voyant...c'mon though, you can't know all that, you must be guessing huh?" "GUESSING?...I'll tell you what Stan, how would you like me to give you a tour of your house right now over the phone? I've never been to your house right?, for that matter not even to your state!" "Right, go for it Max I dare you, I could use a laugh right about now". As Max instantly began speaking, it sounded like her voice was in stereo. It went all around me as she described every room and every piece of furniture in it. I held the phone away from my ear in total silence, stunned by her visit in the spirit. "STAN? Are you still there?" "Yeah Max, hey look, I can't talk anymore right now, give me a minute to compose myself. A lot's been happening around here,...look I'll tell Judy you called and we'll call you back later".

"STAN! What's the matter hon, you don't look so good, you look like you just saw a ghost!" Judy's remarks as she walked in the door at that moment couldn't have been more well timed. "Babe, you had to be here to believe this". "Oh no,...now what Stan?" "Calm down little head, don't get your panties twisted, it's not bad news it's just freaky. Everything is freaky around here just like our old house, I almost can't stand any more of it!" "WELL, what already?" "Max was just here!" "Max was here? I missed her? We haven't spoken to her since last December. Oh no,.. how come she left without waiting for me?" "Look green eyes, she wasn't here physically, she was here in the spirit". "Ok. Stan, now you really have me worried about you, what the hell are you talking about?" "Judy, she called here and we talked for just a few minutes. I told her how depressedI was and she told me about a lot of things we were experiencing". "Soooo....she's a Claire Voyant, that's not unusual, is it?" "Well, at that point I thought she was guessing and dared her to prove what she was saying; before I could say one more word she said she was going to give me a tour of the house and then her voice sounded like it was on stereo speakers all over the place as she went room to room describing every piece of furniture in it!" "So then what happened"? "I had to hang up on the conversation. I told her I needed to lie down and I'd call her back later". "You know something Stan I think we both need to lay down and rest for a while". "I'm with you, I can't really stand much more of this 'spirit' garbage either. Famous last words huh....forget about lying down, the kids just came in."

No sooner had Kurt and Holly entered the house, a police car came screaming up the driveway, lights flashing. **KNOCK, KNOCK**. The officer outside wasted no time jumping out of the car and on to our front porch. "Yes sir" I answered, shaking inside wondering what we were in for now, as if we needed any more bad news. "Look folks" the officer said loudly in a very urgent voice. "A convicted murderer was being transported to a jail in the next town and he escaped. We think he's somewhere around here, so keep your doors locked and don't let anyone in. Call us if you suspect anything!" I quickly shut the door after watching the police car do a quick turn around and race back out of our drive."Great Jude, now we're prisoners in our own house" "Honey, I'll get the kids packed, its Friday....let's go to my mom's home tonight, I don't want to stay here like this. Calling the Police the next day we were told that it was safe to go home but as soon as we entered the house, the same Officer drove up and said to stay in the house until he called back. "What the FRIG is goin' on here Jude? This crap has to stop already!" Within minutes the officer came speeding back and told us that the coast was clear, the murderer had been caught. "By the way officer", I asked in a very snippy response, "What was the name of this guy who got away from you?" "Sir, I don't blame you for feeling the way you do but at least we warned you in time...his name is Frank Bennett"."You're kidding, did you hear that Jude?...the murderer is Frank Bennett....that's the same guy who was a tenant of mine years ago! You know officer, he was a real nice guy back then, wonder what happened to him?" "I don't know, but he won't be crusing around here anymore, see you later". Steve and Elliot arrived soon after and went out to the fort with Kurt in the back of the house. "Mom, Stan, Dad!" they all came shouting and running back in. "There were cigarettes all over the floor of the fort and outside...that murderer must have been hiding out here". Our nerves had just about had it. We were ready to split the whole scene. Watching the landlord later that drizzly day dressed in old boots with his son alongside using a pickax to loosen a clogged drain outside, was the most depressing sight I had seen yet. I looked behind them at the small Christmas Tree farm outside and remembered how we had even taken some presents we put together for less fortunate folks and how, as we drove home that day, we saw a ray of sunshine through the extremely dark clouds, and as we got closer and closer to home how it shined only on our house for a few minutes as we arrived. For one of those rare moments I thought that God might even exist. My more pleasant thoughts were interrupted by the ringing of the phone. Oh God no, please don't let it be Max again. I even wondered at that exact moment why most people say the name of God so much when we don't even believe that He truly exists. "**SAAAN**!" It was Dennis on the other end. "Hey Den, how's things in sunny California?" "SUNNY of course,...whad'ya think...num-nuts?" "How's Jackie do'n" "It was hard for me having her leave here for two weeks vacation to see her mother, where's Judy?" "She's here, she's on the other phone listening". "Hi Jude,...when are you two goin' to get out of Dodge already and come out here with us?" "Boy, I'd sure like to but you know Stan's boys are here, guess we'll be here forever". There was a short silence on the phone line that seemed like forever. "**O.k.**" It was Stan's voice sounding very firm. "O.k?" we said in unison. "Yeah" Stan said again, "O.k., I've had it here, we'll make plans to be out of here by mid September. I think I just got a fill in position in a display company for a few months so we'll have enough extra bucks to make the trip but look, we'll have to stay with you for a few weeks until we can find a house out there". "YOU"RE KIDDING", yelled Den and Jude in unison. "NOPE, not kidding", Stan said again, "See you in September".

"STAN,. what the heck, how are we going to leave Steve and Elliot, San Diego is so far away!" "Judy, I'm at a loss. I can't make a living here and I'm not going to wind up working in an old factory for life. I can't stand all this crazy stuff that's going on anymore and even Max said that if we cross over the three great divides like the Mississippi River then the spirits can't follow. Until they are left behind we can't seem to move on". "Ok. then, how are you going to tell the boys? Plus I have to tell Kurt and Holly's dad too! Stan look, this is a huge decision and I'm scared about what we're doing". "Judy, my heart is breaking right now and I'm at a loss for words but I think that at least if we move we have a chance at a new start in life. Let's just sleep on it Ok?" "Sleep on it?, but you already told Dennis and Jackie's here in town visiting her mother...I'm sure he called her to give her the news". "It doesn't matter Jude, let's just sleep on it like I said". I knew by the tone of Stan's voice that he was stressed so I stayed quiet; not my trait but I learned when to let it go.

"HONEY!" "What Jude?" "The bank called ...they're repossessing our car,...now what do we do"? "Ok., give me a minute; there's gotta be a way out of this. We could hide the car until we leave for California but odds are they'd find it and we'd be hauled into court before we could leave the state. You know, it's really too small to hold all of us and Shabam and the cat and all of our luggage. How 'bout that gal you know ....the one who's husband runs a used car lot". "Yeah, I could call her but Stan if we could buy another car why not just pay off this one?" "Babe, when your friend was at the Disco-Mitzvah her husband admired the two carat diamond ring I had on, even asked about buying it. Maybe he'd consider trading a car for it, you know it's worth a few thousand bucks". "Oh Stan, that was your mom's diamond and you personally designed the gold ring you had it set in,...are you sure you want to do that?" "Well look, it's only a ring and right now we need every dollar we can get our hands on to make this trip out west and don't forget, we still have to pay for a new house rental, food and support until we find jobs there. Call her up and see if we can make an appointment with her hubby. *Has it really come to this?* I thought, as I looked at my one-of-a-kind pinky ring. It was one of the last holdouts of my former wealth besides my expensive Movado watch and my dad's rare Patek Phillipe watch I had inherited. I hurt internally as we bartered the ring for a car. The man pointed out the only car he would consider trading for the ring. It was hardly impressive but it had low mileage and it was clean and big. The six year old four door Dodge was dark brown, ugly and everything I would never have purchased in the past, but it would get us to the west coast safely at least and we had no one to impress anyway. The deal was made and within a few days later the bank's repo people came to the house to pick up our little Mazda. "Whew Stan, that was cutting a little too close for comfort huh?" "Yeah, I know, but at least we own this car outright, no bank involved. I can't even entertain the thought of dealing with a bank anymore. You know Jude; I heard a voice inside me when I lost all of my real estate. It kept repeating over and over and over

"You'll never recover the loss"

It sounded really 'spooky' but I just chalked it up to my own mind talking back to me". "Stan, get that thought out of your head will you? You are still a very smart business man, you just got caught in a financial recession at the time, and you'll make it all back, you'll see". "There she goes again, my "little-head" encourager. If she only knew just how stupid I was feeling over all the dumb mistakes I had made and putting us in this financial position.

(Judy)

Kurt's baby album suddenly appeared on the corner of the dining room hutch one day and the same day Holly's little necklace also re-appeared. She loved that necklace and had looked everywhere for it. I started to look around for Holly's baby book too but it was nowhere. It's funny how you can just dismiss these findings and make up excuses for how they appeared, and that's what I wanted to do but I had no answers. My head was spinning from everything; I needed some fun for a change. "Hey Stan, let's invite Suzanne and Jackie over tonight and play Yahtzee". As Stan talked on the phone, he was laughing for the first time in days. "Jude, you know what they want to know? They want to know if our scary ghost friends are going to play Yahtzee with us?" "Yes, sure, tell them I invited them to dinner too!" We always had a great time with Suzanne and Jackie, especially when they were together at the same place. They had such a funny sense of humor. Suzanne was a little heavy but always looked sharp and laughed a lot, especially about herself. Jackie always sounded like a typical New York telephone operator with her nasal speech, and the jokes they would make about people were harmless but over the top! After they arrived and we had settled down to playing the game for a while the light fixture globe above the table came crashing down in the middle of it in a million pieces. We were all a little high from a few glasses of wine and we all screamed at once. "What the hell just happened", Stan yelled. "Anyone hurt"? "It's one of your frigg'n ghost friends" blurted Jackie, half laughing and half nervous as we all raced out the door to the front porch. Just as we were calming down the outside overhead light exploded. The bulb shattered right from the socket. The girls huddled together for a minute with only the light from the kitchen window lighting up a small area where we were standing. Stan and I were used to the spirits and their crazy games but the girls freaked out. "Hey you guys, we love you but we're getting the frig out of here right now! This place scares the jeebes out of us. STAAN!...walk us to the car. its pitch black out here!" "Well, I told you we'd invite the ghosts to play the game with us, wha'd you expect?" By this time we were all laughing a lot as the girls jumped in the car and sped down the driveway. "Stan, c'mon now that was really freaky. I've never seen that happen before....both lights blowin' out at once? I'm glad the kids aren't here this weekend it would have really freaked them out!" As we cleaned up the mess of shattered glass everywhere, we remained pretty quiet after the gals had left. "Stan? Jackie didn't mention anything about what we told Dennis about us moving to California" "It's Ok., if we go, and it looks like we will, she'll know then, that's for sure" As the days passed I felt very sad. I've moved so many times but this time was different. The thought of taking my children 3600 miles away from their dad and for Stan to leave his precious boys was almost too much to bear. All of the wonderful memories of our meeting and our family fun was here and what children remember. Kurt and Holly were sad and excited at the same time. "Mom", yes

Kurt, "What's going to happen to Steve and Elliot? Why can't they come with us?" "Honey, their mom would miss them but we'll fly them out a lot for visits". "I'm sad to leave Dad. He's really mad and I don't know what to do!" I had no answers for them. It was breaking my heart and all I knew was that time would have to heal all.

"MOM, the Landlord's here!" "Hi Charley what's up"? Charley's face showed his frustration and I knew whatever it was, wasn't good. "I'd like for you and Stan to meet me and my wife at our house. Can you come down at 6 tonight?" "What's this about?", I asked. The kids didn't break anything and the rent was always paid on time but his tone was very threatening. As soon as we entered the house, he started screaming at us. **"ARE YOU MARRIED"?** We both looked at each other and didn't know what to say. "My sister in law works for the Post Office here in town and she wants to know why the names Rose and Charney are always on your mail". I could see Stan beginning to steam. "WHAT? Listen Charley, what right does your sister-in-law have as a Postal employee to discuss our mail with you or anyone"? "WELL", he yelled back again, **"ARE YOU MARRIED?** If not we are ending this lease with you. We are good Christian people and we don't want sin going on in our property". "Look Charlie, we consider ourselves married, we've been together for seven years". "Well that's not good enough for us, we want you out. We'll give you a month to move". **"That's fine with us!"** Stan yelled back as we stormed out of the house. My stomach felt sick and I felt a little bad for Charlie's wife who had sat silently in the room. Our eyes met and neither of us could say a word to diffuse the situation. I guess we really don't have a choice now. I felt *'exiled'* for the second time and we still had to live here and see the owner's every day. "SCREW THEM", Stan said loudly, turning his head back hoping that Charlie heard him. I cried a lot as we walked back up the long drive to our house. "They're "Christians? What kind of Christians talk like that, what are they holier than thou? What a pair of phonies!" The kids wanted to know what happened; they could see that Stan was very angry. I made up some excuse just to brush over the situation with them. Stan's boys visited as much as they could and he clung to them like never before. Oh my God, how did we get here? We fell in love and just wanted a happy life together with our children but here we are. Stan lost all of his properties, lost our business, cars, money, our beautiful home and so much more. I began smoking heavily and Ken gave me some red pills that he said would take the pain away and would make me happy.

We began packing, Jackie and Dennis called every day and our friends Ken and Linda came over to help. Ken had also lost his own business but had found work in an auto parts dealership. He and Stan had become as close as brothers and it was hard for them to say goodbye but Ken and Lin had lived in California years before so from the things they said it looked like they might follow us one day. I looked over on a shelf and saw that stupid red eyed troll and yelled "I'm not taking that demonic thing with us....take it outside and burn it"! "Not me", Stan laughed, "It may start screaming"! "Hey Stan let's just bury it face down somewhere". "Sounds like a plan to me Ken" Stan replied, more relaxed about the situation. I remembered the psychic we had met in this dumpy town who told us in order to keep evil spirits from escaping that you have to make a circle of salt around an object, that way it traps them; so that's exactly what we did and we all felt better when that troll was in the ground. The month passed quickly and moving day had arrived. Stan's ex wife brought Steven and Elliot over to say goodbye. The sadness we all felt was impossible to put into words. Just the thought of leaving his boys brought tears to Stan's eyes and the reality of it was almost too much for him. "Why do you have to go"? cried Elliot. "Son, we have no choice, I can't get much work here and there are a lot of opportunities out in California and besides, I'll fly you and Steven out there to visit a lot". The boys held on to us until it was time to go. My heart broke even more as I saw Stan standing in the middle of the driveway waving goodbye to his sons looking at him through the car's rear window. Kurt and Holly looked on helplessly. They would miss their step brothers a lot. The climax of that day destroyed a piece of our hearts.

***Deceiving spirits had succeeded
in destroying everything we had worked so hard for***

New Beginnings

Chapter 8

NEW BEGINNINGS

(Stan)

As we rolled out of the driveway a million thoughts raced through my mind. With the exception of a few trips out of state and one out of the country to Bermuda on my first honeymoon, my entire life was spent right here in my home state and here I was with my adopted family moving clear across the country to unknown territory. It was exciting and it was scary but it held a lot of promise for a new start. The car was weighted down with its loaded trunk, bikes hanging off of it and a luggage rack with miscellaneous stuff on top....kind of like the "Beverly Hillbillies" on TV. It swayed back and forth with just a touch of the wheel because of all the weight that also included the four of us, Shabam our loyal dog and Sunshine, Holly's cat. Suzanne had located a good owner for Rufus our Sheepdog and although leaving him behind was somewhat upsetting, there really was no room for him and who was going to rent to a family with two dogs and a cat anyway? Shabam and the cat were close buddies by now and got along amazingly well considering the 8 to 9 hrs, 600 plus miles we drove each day for five days. Judy had her little red pills that Ken had given her and I had a bunch of homemade brownies laced with marijuana that Ken had baked especially for me. I kept the stash wrapped in tin foil under my seat and ate some without the kids noticing. I was not about to smoke anything but real cigarettes in front of them. "Hey Hon, after we stop over at your mom's house and finally get going on our trip, I'm really looking forward to seeing Elvis' mansion at Graceland in Memphis. That'll be a real treat huh? "Yes, I guess so". "What's the matter babe, you sound down, maybe you should take one of Ken's 'magic' pills". "It's not that Stan, I'm leaving my mom too you know, this whole move has been pretty nerve racking to say the least" "Yeah, I totally understand but you'll see, new surroundings, new friends a whole new start, who wouldn't want to live in San Diego? You're a warm weather gal; you'll love it there the weather's almost perfect year round!" "You're right, I just need time to adjust, maybe this trip across the country is just what I need, and all that spirit stuff can't follow us either,....right?" Judy's voice was riddled with uncertainty and a whole mix of sadness and happiness. The guilt inside me wanted to rise up for putting us in this position, but pride and deceit about my own abilities kept my mouth shut. How could I have been so deceived over the last six years to have allowed myself to be in such a dumb position? The more I thought about it ...how could I have deceived myself? Forget those thoughts, time for another chocolate brownie, can't change the past right? Oh well, getting a little "high" always seemed to be the right answer or at least it delayed finding out the real truth!

Leaving Judy's mother wasn't easy but off we went. Elvis' mansion was a total bust 'cause it was under repairs. He and his mother were buried side by side out at the pool area which we thought was a little sick. It looked like a three ring circus with souvenirs being sold all over the place in stores outside of Graceland. Judy had relaxed a lot and I was in my total glory with my private stash of brownies. I didn't know which I liked best, the weed inside them or the brownies themselves. A stop over at an Indian reservation in New Mexico was fun and then came Needles, CA the area just before crossing the Mojave Dessert. It was high noon and the temperature was about 100 degrees. We should have waited until late afternoon when the sun started to go down but I didn't want to wait and drove off anyway against the advice of a few folks we met at the crossing. Sure enough, the car's temperature gauge went to 'hot' after only 30 minutes out. I had to turn off the air conditioning and Judy's mom's husband, a former engineer, said that if that happened, to turn on the heater to get the heat out of the engine. All the windows were open, the inside temperature of the car was way over 100 with a hot dessert breeze flowing through. A piece of cardboard blocked the rear window from the sun and our cat jumped into her drinking dish on the floor.

Shabam, tongue hanging out, laid down on the rear seat with Judy and Holly; Kurt was up front with me as I nervously watched the temperature needle hovering between 'hot' and 'almost hot'. I hoped that he wouldn't see my foot shaking a lot on the gas pedal as I looked over a perfectly flat hot dessert road with absolutely no shade whatsoever to stop under. There was one or two overpasses with a bit of shade but the possibility of snakes under them kept me from stopping. I kept talking to Kurt a lot to keep my head straight and away from fearful thoughts. Not one other car ever passed us nor did we ever pass anyone. We were completely alone and the hour or two over the dessert road seemed endless. At last, a gas station with water and shade came into view. The rest of the trip was uneventful but as we got very close to San Diego we passed a car at a stop light which caught our attention. "LOOK STAN isn't that the man we saw in the movie Amityville Horror?" Judy's voice was very deliberate and as I turned to look at the driver he did look amazingly like the real Amityville home owner we had seen. The kids had seen the movie and started to agree with their loud little voices. A shiver rushed over me at the thought of what we had just run away from back home and I shrugged off the possibility of it being true. "Look you guys, I don't even want to think about our past or that stupid movie....Ok?" Judy didn't seem to be very comforted by my response and Kurt and Holly quieted down after a while. It wasn't long before we finally arrived at Dennis and Jackie's house and were back in civilization. "**SAAAN!....JOOOD!**....you look like the 'Beverly Hillbillies'. ..what the frig happened to you?" Our appearance was somewhat frazzled and Jackie hadn't seen us since that last freaky night at the house when the lights blew out but her comments at our arrival was a refreshing moment as she rushed out to see us all practically falling out of the car! Her laughter was contagious and a very welcome sound. God knows, we all needed a lot of laughs that was for damn sure! Who is this God we all quote anyway and why does he keep coming up in my thoughts and my speech? I knew one spiritual realm that was real and I had left it 3600 miles behind us and that was more than enough spirit stuff for me.

(Judy)

Oh my God, it felt so good to see our old friends. I felt so much fear driving over 3,000 miles from home, but I never let Stan see just how much fear I had. Stan had his own issues especially about leaving his sons behind. I really had no idea how this was all going to work out but we were here now and it was time to make the best of it. "Jackie, it's so good to stop moving, especially for the kids and the animals". "I know how you feel Jude, I drove from coast to coast so many times with Kelly and our dog, and I felt like a permanent traveler". "Well...once is enough for me, I'm definitely not one for sitting in a car that long but as long as I had some pills to pop, it got me through it".

After unloading the car and settling in, the kids all ran out and went bike riding with Kelly. Dennis' voice came loudly through the walls from his bedroom. "Hey you two, let's all go in the Jacuzzi for a while". "Oh Den; I've had my eyes on that Jacuzzi since we drove up". As the four of us sank down in the swirling hot water, I felt my body relaxing. For the first time in over a year, Stan and I started to feel prosperity creeping into our lives. We topped off the hour with some wine and a lot of laughs over our past. "Hey Jude, I'm starting to feel like a prune, I'm getting out." "Yeah Stan, you do look a little wrinkled, Jackie and I'll join you .....coming in with us Jude?" "No, I'll be there in a few minutes, I just want to hang here for a bit longer, this is wonderful". I needed my space. I put my head back and thought about what I was missing back home...or was I really just missing the comforts of my familiar life back there? When we had finally arrived in San Diego, it was the end of September and everything looked dead except for the palm trees. I thought it was ugly. New England was quaint and green and full of color most of the months and everything here looked brown. The more I thought about the decision to move, the more frightened I became but the next thoughts I had were about the scary spirits that haunted us back there. I still didn't know what to make of it and started to think about our freedom from it all when we had crossed the three great divides. Everyone told us that those spirits couldn't cross over and that we'd be free of them........**or would we be?** Living with Den and Jackie was difficult for all of us. We were all very independent people who liked our privacy but fortunately we found a house to rent after only a few weeks It was actually the only house available for rent in the area we wanted to stay in because of the good schools there. It was a real step up from anywhere we had ever lived. It was new and it was very large with a huge foyer filled with large plants, a large kitchen, a guest room, an elevated dining area, two recessed living rooms and only several steps up to the three bedrooms over the huge garage. The master bedroom was very large with its own bath and a small balcony overlooking palm trees and hills. It was the end of September and the weather was absolutely perfect. As I looked out over the scene, I was filled with feelings of hope that I hadn't felt in many, many months but I also couldn't help wondering what our future held in store.

(Stan)

It wasn't long before Judy found a job not too far away at a Community Youth Center and I found employment in a Real Estate Signage Company. Our only problem was that we had shipped a lot of our furniture and between rental and living expenses we didn't have enough funds to get it out of storage; so there we were in this gorgeous home sleeping on borrowed air mattresses, a donated couch, table and chairs and a small freezer chest we had to fill with ice daily in place of a refrigerator, but we were survivors and loved living in our elegant new surroundings. My boss was originally from our old home state back east and appreciated my enthusiasm and efforts in his business. When he found out about our circumstances, he co-signed a bank loan so we could start living like normal folks with real furniture once again. The months leading up to 1980 were peaceful and full of excitement and exploration including feeling the effects of a mild earthquake. We were less than an hour from the Bayside Capitol City, park and beach areas and it seemed that our 'spiritual buddies' had actually been unable to cross the three great divides as predicted by some of the clairvoyants and psychics back east....**or so it seemed!**

"STAN"! "Yeah hon what? "Ken and Lin are on the phone, they have something they want to tell you, they sound very excited". "Hi Ken, wha's happen'n friend? "Heyyy bro, its real boring here without you guys. Remember I told you we lived out near San Diego when we were first married?" Yeah, kind a...why? "Well Lin and I have decided to move back west. We're actually all packed, got our van ready...we'll be seeing you in about a week". "NO KIDD'N? Ken....you're really come'n out here?" "I wouldn't joke about that Stan. Hey...you said your house was really large, can we stay with you for a few weeks until we settle in?" "No problemo Senor...see you soon". "WOW Jude, we'll have our two favorite couples out here, won't that be great?" "Ummmm, yes but Stan, remember what Denny said about Ken" "What's that babe?" "You know, he met Ken when he was still living back east and didn't get along with him and he said don't ever bring him to his house and I'm sure that hasn't changed". "Well.... we'll see.....we'll get them together somehow, it'll all work out". "By the way Stan, I met a gal at the Youth Center where I work and she said that the house we're renting is on very old Indian Burial Land, hope there aren't any funny spirits here" "JUDITH!...cut it out, don't get me goin' with this crap anymore!"

By the turn of the New Year, they had arrived and settled in as we had but their short stay turned into a few months and tensions rose between us. I had also hit the age of 40 like a train hitting a brick wall and along with sharing our home for such a long period of time, Judy and I became frazzled. The job I had ended as the company just didn't have enough work for me. Judy also wasn't as happy with San Diego as I was. Our two kids were adjusting fairly well to their new schools and friends, but there were still some challenges with them and I was also feeling deeply the distance between myself and my boys that I had left back home. Emotions flared and we were finding ourselves continually caught up in arguments and finances we didn't know how to handle. Ken and Lin had finally moved out, and before long we realized that we needed to find a less expensive home to rent. In order to do that, I gave our present landlord my expensive solid gold Movado watch as security for the last month's rent with an agreement that I could purchase it back some day. He even offered to lower the rent so we could stay, but a spirit of poverty had gripped me back east and wouldn't let go. The difference of $200 less in rent for the new house was too much of a bargain to pass up. Besides, I was still looking for permanent employment. It was a nice little ranch in the same area as the kid's schools but it reminded me a little of the house we lived in back east and a far cry from the house we just moved out of. But, we were in San Diego and the palm trees surrounding the home kept us from feeling defeated, and we now had financial breathing room with our earnings, but something was still not right in our 'spirits'. There was a feeling of 'being led' rather than just making our own choices. We were determined not to be deceived but we just couldn't put our finger on it and took each day as it came. Kurt and Judy felt very comfortable in our smaller home but Holly and I were upset for a while over leaving the large, beautiful house we had loved so much. "I hope you know Jude how upset I am that I had to give up my beautiful Movado watch to pay the last month's rent to our old landlord so we could move out. I even had to trade my diamond ring for the car so we could get here and now this? When are we ever going to get ahead"? "Hon we're doing what we can". "I know Jude, but it seems like just one road bump after another, it's real discouraging".

(Judy)

I love the Youth Center but there are days I get too involved with the precious children. Today was really hard; I had to walk across the street with an 8 year old little boy whose mother didn't pick him up. When we entered his house, the mother was no where in sight, lights didn't work and he introduced me to his huge Python (snake). Mamma was off at the bar and he was alone as he said he was for many nights and was scared. I had to report it to the authorities because I cared too much for his safety, but there was nothing more that I could do.

"Stan, there's a street fair going on up in Alpine near the Youth Center today and tomorrow, lots of booths and entertainment, let's go to it". "O.k., O.k, sounds real boring but what the heck! Are there going to be sheep and old fire engines there too?, I can hardly wait!" "Hey look Stan, it's free....we don't like it we'll leave". The kids were busy with their friends so off we went to the fair......Big Mistake! "Stan, Stan, look over there!" "Oh what already? I told you this would be boring". "No Stan, check it out...it's a hand writing expert". "Get real hon, they can't possibly tell what someone's personality is just by their handwriting crap, it's just another scam". "Oh lighten up Stan; I'm going to do it!" The lady at the booth was so sweet. She was tall with short blonde hair. "Hi, do I know you? I'm Ms Zoble. You look like a June or a Judy". "What? Are you psychic?" "Not exactly, I do mostly hand writing analysis; ...would you like me to do yours?" I looked at Stan; he had this 'whatever' look on his face" "Go ahead...maybe she can tell me something I don't know about you". "WOW Stan, .check this out. She has me really pegged....she described me to a 'T'. JOYFUL, ALWAYS BUBBLY, DEPENDABLE, LOVING.....LOTS OF FEAR, LOTS OF PAIN". Stan leaned over close to me and whispered "That's all pretty easy to tell about you hon, but look at the psychic stuff thrown in, this woman knows a lot more than she is saying". The lady looked at us with a smile that suggested some immediate action on our part. "You know folks; I have more in depth classes I hold at my house near where you live. We're having a meeting this coming Tuesday night at 7pm would you like to attend? There's no charge, just sit in and observe". Stan answered instantly. "Maybe, give us your address and phone number, we'll call you". When we left, we felt excitement but also some hesitation at the same time.

Tuesday came and we decided to go and quickly discovered that it was actually a handwriting school located in San Francisco. "Stan and Judy you could really learn a lot at the next meeting, and by the way, there really is no charge but the school does accept donations of any amount". We looked at each other and felt very drawn to attend.

The class was fascinating and far more than we could have imagined. Our curiosity had taken us over as usual. Little did we know that the "Veil of Deception" was once again clouding our thinking and decision-making. We we're still desperately searching for the real truth of life. A week went by. We were excited and nervous at the same time and couldn't wait for the meeting to happen. "Hi guys", Ms Zoble said as she greeted us with her slender arms outstretched, "I'm so glad you could come tonight, we have a full house, just find a seat somewhere. You're in for a real treat". The first meeting had only about five people present but one of the directors of the school from San Francisco was there and there was only standing room for those who arrived late. As we sat, listened and watched there were things happening that we had never seen before. The teacher looked straight at me and said in a very encouraging tone "Judy...how about you taking part in an experiment to show everyone the energy force and power we all have in our minds?"

Hmmm...I thought this was supposed to be just a continuation of the handwriting class...oh well,...what the heck, I'm game!

I had no clue what this guy was talking about. "Come here and sit in this chair" *Uh, OH!..the chair was in the middle of the room....what's this a hot seat?* I looked at Stan and did what the teacher said, everyone's eyes glued on me. "Now class, I'm going to show you the energy force you all have inside of you. I want you to focus on Judy and let it all pour out of you". He motioned to two men to stand beside me and he had them put two fingers each under both of my armpits and then told them to visualize lifting me off the chair. I heard strange music in the background and instantly felt myself in another state of mind as I felt myself levitating off the chair with just their fingers under my armpits. I was actually floating in the air. The next thing I felt was a slow lowering back on to the chair. When I opened my eyes, everyone clapped; I looked over at Stan with his mouth hung open. The class went on a bit longer and then we left. After getting in our car I looked at Stan. "What the heck just happened to me?" "Jude, I don't know but when I saw you levitating, it really scared me. We ain't goin' back there ever!" I agreed with him and we rarely talked about that evening again.

(Stan)

"Hey Jude, we're going to pick up Ken and Lin and go to DJ's our favorite disco nightclub. "Wow Stan that sounds great, I love that place but it's expensive to buy drinks there". "Hey, you and Lin leave the bottle of wine home, we're going to go out and just enjoy ourselves and listen Judy, **for once...stop worrying about the money will ya**"? I felt an argument coming on and it did. We tried to pretend we were happy when we picked up our friends but they could tell something was wrong, and they were also having their own issues. What was causing all this confusion that was separating us, I couldn't stand it anymore. All I could think of that night was the position of display manager I had been interviewing for with one of the largest department store chains in California. I was never intimidated about applying for a job I knew relatively little about. I figured that if I could wrangle my way in the door, I would learn all I could about the job quickly and fake it 'til I made it, so when I found out that the huge clothing chain of May Company was looking for a display manager at their Fashion Valley Mall store I jumped right on it. After all, I did have display experience with our former jewelry business as well as some community theater set designing and costumes during the years with my ex wife. Linda even went with me one day to search out what mannequins were all about in stores and a few manufacturers. I got a quick education about the different types of mannequins and surprisingly enough, I competed for the job and was scheduled for a final interview to be hired, even after breaking off an arm of one of the mannequins while trying to dress it. I thought for sure I had the job, so at DJ's that night I grabbed the mike and asked Judy to marry me. I thought that would be very dramatic and she would like it. Embarrassed by all the attention focused on her she said yes but later that night after returning home she threw the temporary ring I had bought on the ground and screamed at me like a woman possessed. I was no wimp, that's for sure and frustrated and rejected I yelled right back at her. We were still outside and I was sure our neighbors got an earful but I could have cared less. What had happened to us since we met? There were days as if nothing had changed and other days where everything had changed between us.

The position at May Company fizzled and I found myself working once more in another job I had little or no experience in. It was delinear drafting with a company right in town, and I had convinced the manager that I had a lot of experience back east. It was a Friday that I got hired and by the next day, I checked out a number of books from the library and studied everything I could about the subject. I had watched my ex-partner Dennis as he prepared a lot of architectural drawings but he never actually did that many delinear drawings which were much more detailed showing cabinetry and walls sliced open from the side. Monday came quickly and after an extensive tour of the offices, I sat nervously on my first day on the job, surrounded by several expert draftsmen. I stared blankly at the huge layout paper taped to the board in front of me without a clue as to where to start. I thought that since it was almost noon that I would just sneak out to lunch and never return. As the men left for lunch, they invited me to go with them, but I excused myself for some phony reason and just kept staring at the blank paper in front of me. All of sudden it was like a light bulb was turned on in my head and I began to prepare the drawing which needed to be completed that day. Although I had a few similar past drawings as references, I was absolutely amazed that my work was returned to me with only five small errors on it at the end of the day. Each day had fewer errors and by day four there were none. There must be a God somewhere I thought, 'cause I could hardly believe that I could do this complicated work at all; but as my luck would have it, after six weeks or so, the company lost some contracts and since I was the last to be hired, I was the first to be let go.

"What the hell is goin' on already?
I get complemented and thanked for doing great work and then this company loses its contracts just like my former employer. Is it me or what? Did those spirits manage to follow us after all? My life frigg'n sucks. It's like being on a permanent rollercoaster. I can hardly face my wife, kids and friends anymore"!

The summer went by fast. Steve and Elliot flew out to visit and our family was once again united. Every weekend we would all relax on San Diego's gorgeous beaches with Steve and Kurt, as usual, running off forever exploring, and Judy, Holly, Elliot and I staying close to each other with walks and castle building. I had found work with a temporary employment agency which sent me to different assignments but at least that kept me fully employed which, in turn, helped settle our anxiety over finances and also helped keep our relationship on track. During daytime hours we were the perfect example of upstanding, happy, concerned, normal parents; at night however, we led a double life; a totally different couple winding up a lot of nights at Den and Jack's house. Ken and Lin were sometimes with us as but they were still mostly our dance partners at the many clubs still offering disco nights. Den and Jack always had good pot in stock as well as something they called "shrooms". Shrooms were the kind of mushroom that when chewed on made you laugh nonstop. We were no strangers to nude bathing and would often go to San Diego's famous Black Beach to swim. The sensation of swimming naked in the ocean was best compared to total freedom.....maybe the closest thing to floating around in a mother's womb! So, it was very natural to find us doing much the same in their Jacuzzi, sipping wine and me smoking some good pot. Their rented home was perched pretty high up on a hill and as we relaxed in the hot swirling water, we could stare up at a star filled sky and also see out over the surrounding hills and valleys filled with thousands of night lights. There was nothing like it. We were always overjoyed to be able to go to their place and escape our boring lives. Dennis and Jackie were the most uninhibited people we had ever met so we thoroughly enjoyed each and every opportunity to get together. Somehow, those months softened Judy's heart and mind about marriage. We even managed to take a trip up the coast to Big Sur where my ex-brother and sister-in-law lived and had built an extraordinary home from two interconnected huge wine vats. The woods, hills and beaches surrounding Big Sur were sensational and romantic and Judy finally agreed to get married. I was still looking around at beautiful female bodies and I was sure that Judy had fantasies of her own; we were in our forties with hormones still raging and changing, so we just chalked it up to normal lust. Steve and Elliot had flown home and we were finally at peace with each other and with life as it happened day by day.

(Judy)

I started to really think a lot more about my life. I was always a good girl growing up with good morals, a virgin when I first married...but where did it all get me? I knew underneath it all what the right thing to do was, but all my life people had promised me things and rarely delivered. I believed them and I always wanted to please everyone, even now, but if I go back to the person I was with my first husband I will never keep Stan. We both wanted and needed to explore life but most everyone we knew or met live day by day hoping and wishing for excitement but never achieving it. I looked in the mirror at who I had become and realized for the first time that I could never go back. There was too much adventure in me. I found myself shouting *God help me!* I knew the proper thing to do was to get married, especially if I wanted to keep Stan. He was determined not to go on with me always being a Charney and I knowing it was a lazy way out. I knew that there were many women just waiting for the opportunity to grab Stan from me. *Okay God...if you're up there I'll get married...if that's your best plan then help me to make it mine!* As time went on, marriage seemed the way to go. I began to get excited and finally told Stan how I felt and shortly after that we began to make plans to fly back to our little New England town and reserve a date for the wedding at the local diner where we hung out every day for lunch. It was just a few blocks down the street from Stan's office and would be perfect for a small crowd of friends and a few relatives. Stan was able to hire a Pastor there that was a personal friend of ours.

"Honey, how 'bout we marry right after Christmas on the 28th? We wanted to go back and visit the boys for the Holidays....it would be a perfect time don't you think?" "Babe, the sooner the better; I'll make all the flight reservations and talk to Norman about reserving the diner...I think the 28th is on a Sunday so it just may work out and I'll also get in touch with our friend Pastor Jim". I could see all the excitement on Stan's face.

It was a good decision and I don't know if it was God or not...
but it sure seemed like it!

As the time grew closer we got really excited for Christmas and Chanukah but especially for our wedding and our return to the little town where we met. I felt that I had better tell my boss Michelle at the youth center where I worked that I would need the time off. I put in so many extra hours that I thought it shouldn't be too hard. Boy was I wrong! My boss also wanted the same time off and no matter how much I explained about our wedding her answer to me was... "you leave...you don't come back!" I was crushed. Stan was still working with a temp agency so he had no problem, but now it was all up to me. "Judy...QUIT and quit right now! She has used you over and over again. YOU are the one the kids enjoy and love at the center and she has always been jealous of you over that. This is an important day for us. You know hon, with your knowledge and talent you won't have any problem getting another job and a better one at that, but not until we come home from the wedding!" I was happy that Stan was so encouraging. I was a hard worker and still had a problem with standing up for myself but I finally faced Michelle and said the words....*I QUIT, I QUIT, I QUIT!!!* Whew! It felt good to finally tell her off...I had had enough of her bullying. She was a very funny boss, nice one minute and mean the next but when I said the words QUIT....she became more humble than I had ever seen her before. No matter how much she tried to keep me there I looked straight at her and said "So...I can have the week of Christmas off, right?" She still wouldn't go for it and didn't believe me so I said it once more... **"I QUIT!"** As I left the building, I turned and saw her starring at me in absolute shock and silence. I felt a little bad for her but it sure felt good to be in charge of my life for a change.

I wanted the wedding to be very casual so I picked out a pair of gray slacks, a pink angora sweater and a white angora hat. I was never one to be fancy and although when I had first met Stan he was a lot more formal, he had also become a lot more relaxed and dressed in white pants and a pull over mauve colored velour sweater. My family said they couldn't attend due to the distance they lived and since I had lived with Stan for seven years, they said it was only a ceremony and they saw us as married anyway. So I had only my children and our friends. Stan had his boys and his cousins who he had introduced to each other at the time of his first marriage. Kurt and Holly went to stay with their dad after the wedding and Stan's boys went home to their mother's house. Since we didn't have enough money for two nights in a hotel we stayed with a friend the first night and then drove to New York City for the second night for a return romantic memory. When I woke up the next morning, I looked over at Stan and then at my ring finger and realized for the first time that I was actually now Mrs. Judy Rose. WOW....even though we had lived together seven years, it still felt different to be one with Stan....his WIFE! Honeymooning in New York for a day and a half was really fun and then a short trip back to New England to pick up the kids and take them out to visit our old house. We all shared a lot of memories but after a while we began to feel very strange and uncomfortable. We all knew that this was the reason we had to move. As we walked up the long dirt driveway, we felt the same strange spirit we had experienced while living there. "MOM", yelled Kurt, "Let's get out of here!" Holly got tears in her eyes and we knew that as much as we loved the house, that we could never go back. Such a beautiful house but such a powerful force of darkness we couldn't explain. We all looked at each other, got back into the car and headed for the airport, stopping off to say goodbye to Steve and Elliot which was hard on all of us but especially hard on Stan.

Arriving back in San Diego, we were met by our friends greeting us as Mr. & Mrs. Rose. It didn't take us long to run down to the City Hall to register our Marriage License but we quickly found out that it wasn't legal since I didn't have my birth certificate from New York for the ceremony like you're supposed to. It wasn't legal? *Whatever*, as the kids were saying now, I ordered the certificate from New York and that took a few more weeks. I never told anyone about it, we just pretended to get the license. To me it was just one more stupid piece of paper. "HEY STAN", I joked, "I'm single again...cool... I still have more time to think about this whole marriage thing". "OH NO YOU DON'T sweet cheeks, we'll just wait for the papers and go down to the Wedding Chapel downtown and re-do the ceremony on February 7th..but...our marriage will always be December 28th!" *Oh my*, I thought....*what a screwed up life we live.* I couldn't stop my mind from wandering back to the last day when we visited our old house.

I hope the spirits didn't follow us and attach them to us again,
I thought... I could definitely feel fear rising up my legs
to the pit of my stomach!

Marriage was still so new to me. I couldn't stop looking at my ring; Stan is really my husband now. I never dreamt that I would have such a connection of oneness in all the years we lived together. Hmmm....must be something to this marriage thing. On the one hand I felt absolute joy and on the other hand fear. I decided that I'd better leave my thoughts on the happy hand and move on. Well, the time had come that I had to start hunting for work after we returned from our wedding. I felt a little excitement and I needed a change and a challenge, and a challenge I got!

"STAN!... I got the job with the Solar Roofing Company in La Mesa...the next town over. He wants me to start right away". "That's great babe, I'm so proud of you but we do have a small problem, we only have one car and my job is in Kearny Mesa, how are we going to work this out? Our hours are not be the same!" "Oh crap-itas, I never thought of that". "It's Ok. doll, I'll take you the first day so I'll be just a bit late! ...ya know..the first day is always a bit nerve wracking anyway...you need to check in early".

As I was getting familiar with the company and being in charge of all the sales reps and their schedules, I was also starting to feel a little uncomfortable about the owner of the company. When I went to his office to have him sign some docs, I smelled alcohol. *Oh, I guess he just had a little too much at lunch, I thought.* The more time that went on, the more uncomfortable I felt around him. He was mellow when I was interviewed but now he was crude and rude and he also had a vocabulary that even made ME blush! Whew, first day over with. I was glad that Stan was going to pick me up but I really had to find a better way for me to get to work after that. When I got home I checked with the bus company and found out their schedule. "Okay Stan, this is what I'll have to do....I'll take my bike to Main St, lock it up and take the bus near to where I work, it's only four blocks from the bus stop". "WHAT?...are you sure Jude?" "Do I have a choice"? The next day was a little difficult but I made it to work on time with 15 minutes to spare. I didn't want to complain but there was something definitely wrong with this company. I loved the guys I was working with but felt very uneasy about my boss, Mr. Traci. Every morning when he walked through the door I felt intimidated. He was always inebriated, yelling and staggering. The guys could handle it but I felt uncomfortable especially when he threw things at me to work on. There weren't too many kind things he could say. "JUDY...come in here quick", his voice was rough and growled a lot when he yelled. "I want you to be in charge of hiring and firing and hear me...if these salesmen aren't cutting it you are to fire their asses or your ass will be out of here too...got it? I'm hiring another gal to assist you but you're in charge!" I didn't know whether to be happy or be in fear. "Thanks Mr. Traci, I'll handle it!" As I went back to my desk, my knees were shaking. *This is my boss?....rude, crude and drunk? As Stan would say sometimes....**OY VEY!*** I enjoyed the girl he hired. Her name was Joyceline, Joy for short. We got along great. We called ourselves the 'The Hire Fire Girls'. The salesmen came and went like they were going through a revolving door. I hated when I had to let someone go but it was all about sales and I did my best to help anyone I hired to perform. There was one salesman in particular I liked a lot. Tim was quite tall and energetic and a great salesman. We always played tricks on each other. On one occasion I set an appointment for him and told him he was to go and check out their roofing. Joy and I worked hard at keeping a straight face. We sent him to a nudist camp in the woods. We couldn't wait for him to return. "JOY!...Tim's back, let's not say a word, let's pretend we are innocent!" "Hi Tim, how'd it go?" "GREAT", he answered loudly as he walked into the back office. There was total silence. *Did he really go on the assignment we wondered?* A few minutes passed and we heard a lot of laughter coming from the back office as Tim told some of the other guys all what had happened. "OKAY YOU TWO, get in here! I gotta say that was the wildest trick you have played on me so far, or anyone for that matter! I drove up to the outside gate and rang the bell and waited a bit for someone to come out and let me in. As the man opened the gate, he didn't have one stitch of clothes on. As I told him who I was, he explained that they sure didn't need my services". "Did you get inside Tim?" "NO, he stopped me and told me to u-turn and leave. I felt a little embarrassed and left.....although it could have been better if he would have been a she, I guess I would have lingered a bit longer! I'll get even with you two one day, you are too much!" "Hey Joy, at lunch could you run me over to the bank to cash my check?" "Sure, but are you serious,...there's not enough money in the account to cover our checks yet". The bank teller was so sweet, she checked and double checked. "Sorry Mrs. Rose but there's not enough funds to cover even one of your checks". "JOY? What the hell is happening here? I'm pissed...I'm going to find out from that drunk what's goin' on". Mr. Traci wasn't at the office when we returned. The more I waited for him, the more nervous I got. Just then I saw his car pull up and watched as he staggered into the office. "Mr. Traci, I need to talk to you". "Oh yeah? What?" he answered in his usual rude voice. "Well, I'll tell you what sir, our paychecks bounced that's what!" I felt my legs shaking a bit as I answered him back. "Oh... I forgot to make a deposit; I'll go do it now". He was in a terrible mood, screaming at everyone. He looked like he had slept in his clothes and stunk like a drunken sailor. What the heck was I doing in a place like this? I hate this job and I'm always frightened around him...he gives me the creeps! The next day we went back to cash our checks and it was the same story...no money! We both decided to wait it out to the end of the week and try again. It was getting really bad in the office, we were hiring people and in a week they were quitting....no one liked the atmosphere. We tried once more to cash our checks with no result and when that happened, a light bulb went on. I figured a way to get our money and get the hell out of there. Tim helped us out and we called one of the customers who had signed up for a solar roofing but hadn't quite paid for the whole job. Joy and I went over to see her and talked her into paying half of what she owed at a 10% discount. She agreed, we deposited the money, cashed our paychecks and ran back to the office. Thank God Mr. Traci wasn't there which gave us the chance to go through the files and pull out all of our individual paperwork, changed our addresses, phone numbers and Social Security Numbers so he could never contact us. Out went the lights with a 'snippy' goodbye note, locked the door, dropped the keys through the slot and never returned. *What a job from hell, I'm glad I never have to be around that maniac drunk anymore!* Oh well...here I am...jobless again, but relieved and happy. "Hi hon, you look a little strange tonight, anything wrong?" "Not really babe, I quit the job and I got my money!" "YOU QUIT?. you're kidding?" "Yes, but hold on I've got some really good news also". After I told Stan about what happened with the paychecks and Tim's assignment, we were in hysterics over the nudist colony episode and wished we could have been right there at the gate to see Tim's face! "STAN guess what, I got a call from the Nursery job I applied for as soon as I got home and they want me to start immediately!" "Oh yeah..the plant nursery, what's the position?" "Secretary and it pays good with a lot of benefits. I'm finally stepping out to improve myself. Remember the first job I was offered at Balboa Park? I can't believe they wanted me that badly and they were even willing to pay the employment fee and still hire me even when my shorthand was so rusty". It was such a big job as an event coordinator and I would have worked with the top people at the park. I let fear over-rule my decision and settled for what I was familiar and comfortable with. I was afraid of failure. Wow, the pay was double what I made at the Youth center! "Hey hon, I always told you, you are smart and people love your personality, but all you have to do is conquer those fears that have held you back".

Desperate Searching

Chapter 9

DESPERATE SEARCHING

(Stan)

As I awoke from a restless sleep, I realized it was a day of celebration...of sorts. It was my birthday...or was it? It was the 28th of February but I was born on a leap year and my birthday was on the 29th which really only made me 10 and 1/4....so I could argue that point with everyone; after all,......I only would have had 10 and 1/4 real birthdays.....but...hey...so, I was 41..I felt great and looked young so who cares! The ring of the phone shocked me. "**Stan?**", it was the voice of John, the guy who interviewed me for a Marketing position at May Centers, owners of a new Mall to be opened called Plaza Bonita. "You're hired for the job!" John's voice was loud and excited as he gave me the news. I could hardly believe what I was hearing. My silence for the first few seconds left John a little concerned. "Hey Stan....what's up...you could show a little more enthusiasm....cat got your tongue or what?" "Sorry John, it's Saturday and I just wasn't expecting your call...it kind of took my breath away....OH YEAH....I'm very excited!" "Good, that's better....you had me worried....it was hard to tell from your delayed response....come in Monday at 9 so we can get the paperwork started and be ready to start your new duties..O.k....there's a lot to do!" "I am really jazzed John, be there at 9, see you then". "Stan....who was that?, Judy asked, her green eyes sparkling with the early morning light that streamed through the open blinds as we both sat motionless in the bed. "I GOT THE JOB", I yelled, as I jumped up in total amazement of what had just happened. "You mean the Plaza Bonita job.....is that right?" "Oh yeah babe, we are on our way to financial success and this is the biggest challenge I've ever had, that's for sure". "I'm with you hon....you can do it...you can do anything you set your creative mind to do...that's for sure".

Within an hour the phone rang again. This time with more news I could hardly contain. "DAD!" it was Steven my oldest son's voice on the phone. "I've decided to come live with you and Judy is that O.K."? "**O.k** **are you kidding?**....I said, absolutely stunned by his statement and question. "Of course it's O.K.....when are you coming out here"? "Well, I figured right after school lets out...but do you have a room for me"? "Ummm, I tell you what Steve, we moved into a smaller ranch home with only three small bedrooms but I'll construct a room for you in our sunroom until we can figure something out". "That sounds alright dad, can't wait to see you again". "How 'bout Elliot"? "Oh, Elliot's fine with the plan...he can't wait to get our bedroom all to himself an get me off his back, besides he'll come out with me for the summer and return back before school starts. "Stevie, can't wait to see you and Ell again ...hey...summer's not too far away, get packin'...I'll get the airline tickets reserved as soon as you give me the dates O.K.? "Judy....can you believe this day? We are going to go out and celebrate for sure. Hey, I have an idea...it's raining out...how 'bout we get out of here and go to our mall and buy some new clothes and maybe have a nice lunch somewhere?" "All right Stan...now you're talkin'....be ready in a jiff." It felt so good to see my wife excited over the prospects of a new future for a change....and...she was now my wife...as well as my lover and best friend......what could be better?

My head was still spinning as we drove into the parking lot singing along to Frank Sinatra's song...*I did it my way.* **C R A S H**....the sound was deafening as our car was hit from the side by an oncoming small pickup truck speeding down the aisle we were crossing. It hit us on the driver side and the impact sent me sliding into Judy's side pushing her into the door and spinning the car completely around. In just a moment of time, our singing went to stunned silence. "Are you O.K. babe?" "Yeah, I think so...what just happened? Where'd that truck come from?" "I don't know, but his whole front end is smashed....he's not going anywhere. As I looked over the situation from the outside, it looked like our car could be driven but the guy's truck was totaled. Within minutes we both realized that neither of us was insured so....he was on his own and it wasn't bad enough that our car was not exactly the best looking wheels in town it now looked like it was in a demolition derby.

After sending my wife into the mall to get out of the rain and rest up for a while, I proceeded to pry out the fender a little so the rear wheel could move freely. "**SIR**", the male voice loomed loudly next to me. "IS THIS YOURS?" "Is what mine?" I asked frustrated as I feverishly kept working on the crushed fender. The uniformed Mall policeman was holding a small bag of something in his hand and as I attempted to grab it from him...he swung his hand away and said..."SIR....you'll have to come with me...this bag contains marijuana....I found it right next to you on the ground. Within minutes I found myself handcuffed and led to the Mall Guard's Office. After some time of arguing with the chief, I was let go. I knew it was my bag but they couldn't prove it and were forced to free me. What was even worse was that the accident had happened right in front of a May Company Store, owned by May Centers my new employer. My accident and phony arrest sent a chill though my mind. *Suppose my new employer found out? What the hell, I thought, how could such a great day turn out to be such a mess?*

I spent the rest of the weekend in shifting moods from joy to worry over the possibility of my new employer finding out about the accident and my arrest by the mall police. On top of it all I was totally embarrassed to be driving such a piece of junk now and parking it far from the entrance to the offices out of sight from my employer. The paperwork was completed without any problems and the mall accident was never discovered so I was home free.

My chief boss and the person in charge of the entire pre-opening of the new mall turned out to be Elaina who, as it was revealed to me by my newly appointed secretary, had literally slept her way to the top and knew relatively nothing about management except what she had book learned. She had little or no people skills and as time went on I discovered that she was disliked and distrusted and even hated by some people on her staff and just about anyone else connected with the project, save for the VP she was involved with and a few of her female pet managers of other May Center stores. I worked hard, learned the ropes fast and successfully completed any task thrown at me. Elaina had a very strange marriage. Her husband, of who knows how many years, came to visit her once a year from New York and she in turn traveled back east on occasion as well. Otherwise, their personal lives were their own and even mutually agreed to. It didn't take long for me to find out that my boss John was also under her 'spell' and did everything to appease her. She dressed kind of frumpy and although basically a friendly sort, demanded her instructions to be followed without question often quoting the company manual and other industry publications. Common sense was not her best attribute that was for sure.

"Stan, come into my office for a minute I want to show you something". Elaina's voice always sent chills up my spine. I never knew what kind of mood she'd be in but I was always prepared to let her think that she knew what she was talking about. As I entered her office, she closed the door and asked me to sit down with her on the couch instead of her sitting behind her desk and me in front as usual. I noticed that she looked rather sexy that morning. Instead of a blouse buttoned up to her neck, it was un buttoned and open to her cleavage. As she sat down, she pulled her skirt up to her knees and moved closer to me as she unfolded photos and information on the table in front of us. I had to admit, she had nice legs and she was pretty sexy looking for a change. "Stan", Elaina said in an unusually soft voice, "You know, I have so many things to discuss about the pre opening ceremonies of the mall that there really isn't enough time during the day to discuss it all. How about meeting me for dinner tonight after work so I can explain it all to you?" I knew that she had her eyes on me for a while and had a plan to seduce me as she had with John. John had often let it be known that he, Elaina and some friends often got together in Crest, a mountain top community for parties. Her home also had a Jacuzzi and it didn't take too much imagination to know that drugs were available. "Thanks Elaina", I answered with no hesitation, "I have a wife and family to get home to but I can stay a little later after work here in the office if that will work for you". Elaina's mood changed real fast. "Well Stan, your wife will have to play second fiddle to your job". "Sorry Elaina, but that's the way it has to be". "O.k. then, just take all of this info and get back to me tomorrow and tell me what you think. See you then". Elaina pulled her skirt down and walked quickly back to her desk.

What an evil bitch! I thought. There's no way she'll ever get those hooks into me! I had made a permanent enemy in my own camp, but I'll outsmart her for sure! Or so I thought

The pre opening event went off without a hitch. The construction workers raised the final beam with a small tree on top as usual. The Mayor of the town and other officials were present as well as the press and other media. The theme song was played for the first time, totally unexpected by Elaina and John. I had produced a spectacular event and was congratulated by everyone. Within a few weeks, construction inside the mall was in full swing and I noticed something which needed immediate attention but something which also needed approval by the company executives. Elaina was meeting with them at their head offices out of state when I called and spoke to the Vice President whom I had met on several occasions. When Elaina returned she had my boss come to my mobile office outside the mall that very morning. "Stan", John said with a sad look on his face, "Elaina sent me in to tell you that you are fired and you need to leave here this morning" "FIRED…what in the world for?" "Well, she said that you hadn't been in contact with the local auto agency as she asked you to do and that you didn't talk to her first about the changes inside the mall before you talked to the Vice President". "THAT BITCH! O.K. John, I'll leave but you tell her this for me, she hasn't heard the last of me…She'll regret her decision and so will you". True to my words, I let the President know what had happened as well as a lot of personal information I had about Elaina and John along with my intention to sue for sexual harassment. Within a few weeks, actually to my surprise, I received a call from the Vice President telling me how sorry they were about the situation and asked what they could do to satisfy me if I would refrain from bringing them to court. Hey, all I wanted was my job back and fire that evil witch Elaina. I really enjoyed what I was doing more than anything I had ever been involved with in my entire life. "We're sorry Stan, we can't do that" was the answer I didn't want to hear as I fumed quietly on the other end of the phone. "In that case sir, see you all in court" I answered back firmly. I guess he took me seriously and within a few weeks I found out that both Elaina and John were also fired as well. My lawsuit threat against May Centers consumed me. I could hardly believe what had happened, especially losing an unbelievably wonderful job I could hardly wait to go to every day. Anger filled me to a point I hadn't ever felt before and I didn't know quite how to handle it. How can I possibly tell Judy about this?

Those friggen spirits must be after me again, I thought.
I may as well just stay at temp jobs; I can't seem to build a future
for myself. I feel like a complete failure!
What the hell am I doing wrong?

(Judy)

My new boss at the Nursery was Jerry. He was the complete opposite of Mr. Traci. Jerry was thoughtful and helpful during the first few weeks of my getting used to the work load. He never used foul language or yelled. He was also quite tall and handsome. He was trim like Stan and had light blonde hair. It was such a restful change from my former nightmare boss. "Judy can you come over here for a minute"? "Sure, I'll be right there Jerry". I loved my job at the nursery and the people I worked with and I especially liked my boss. I knew that Stan was a little jealous of him but....oh well! "Look Judy, instead of billing Len's Nursery...let's barter the plants...I need work done on our tractors and he can help us". "You mean the entire order or just a part of it". "Do the whole amount; we need a lot of work done on our equipment". Jerry's suggestion got me real excited. I loved the bartering system and I loved Jerry's creative business mind.

"Hey Judy", Jerry yelled as I left his office, "We're all going over to Chuck and Carol's for pizza tonight why don't you join us"? "Mmmmm...what time"? Just the possibility of getting together socially sparked something in my spirit that I thought was dead. "Well...around 5:30 or so...right after work". Chuck and Carol owned the nursery and I got along really good with both of them. "Sounds great Jerry...O.K., count me in". Calling Stan at work so he could meet me there I was greeted with a short pause from the operator. "Who's calling please?" "This is his wife, is Stan there?" "I'm sorry Mam but he doesn't work here any longer". "WHAT?...since when"? "Since yesterday, sorry"! As I hung up the phone, I was shocked. Is that why he's been so quiet ...wonder what's happened now? I could feel so many emotions erupting inside me and so many questions popping up. As the day passed I could feel anger building. Why didn't he tell me, what's all this secret stuff going on with him lately? I decided to go to Chuck and Carol's house alone. The thought of going home got me very upset. Jerry knew something was wrong and began questioning me. "Judy, what's up girl? You're awfully quiet and that's definitely not like you". I took one look at Jerry and my eyes filled up with tears. I wanted so much just to curl up in his arms for comfort but he was my boss. He just held my hand for comfort. I could feel the tears flowing and I was fighting with everything I had to be strong but I wasn't winning. "Jerry, I called Stan's company and found out that he wasn't working there any longer ..and that's as of yesterday...but he never told me!" Jerry tried to sweeten the pie by explaining a man's side of the situation but he didn't know that this had become Stan's track record. It seemed to be following him with every job. I just thanked Jerry, put a smile back on my face and changed the subject. It was 7pm and I decided that it was time to head home to my family or they would begin to worry. They knew I worked late some nights but now I felt an urge to get back quickly. I'm so afraid to face Stan 'cause he's obviously going through his own hell but I still feel such anger over his silence and this pattern of losing jobs.

Before leaving I met Corrie, a gal I worked with. She was a bit younger than me but we had a lot of laughs together. I called Stan and told him that Corrie and I were going out for a while before coming home and that I would be home late. That was a big mistake. Corrie knew I felt unhappy and that Stan and I were started having some problems. "Hey Judy, I've got something to make you forget your problems". "Oh yeah Like what...a bundle of money?" I watched as she pulled out a plastic baggie from her purse. It was filled with what looked like white powder. "And may I ask...what is that?" My gut feeling was not to ask any more questions but my curiosity got the best of me.

"It's what we call the happy drug, it's called crystal; it'll make you forget your troubles...at least for a while anyway". I had worked with teens years ago back home and knew what drugs could do but I wanted to stop the pain. .Trembling inside I asked, "Corrie...how do we do this?" I watched as she found and pulled out a small mirror and emptied the powder onto it and with a tiny straw divided it into little rows and began sniffing it up her nose. The sight of it made me very nervous and I became very scared. "Corrie, I've never done anything like this before". "O.K. Judy, I won't pour so much just try a little". Curiosity still had me in control so I agreed. "WOW!...that stuff really burns your nose...how do you stand it Corrie?" "Hey, don't worry, you'll feel the effects real soon and you'll feel real good". She was right, in a few minutes my cares and worries disappeared and I felt really happy for the first time in a long while. Boy, this stuff really relieves tension but I knew that it would also change my personality when the high dropped. Things had eased up a bit financially with our new jobs and we had managed to buy another car to make it easier on us and to give Stan a better feeling about himself. As I pulled up to the house I saw Stan's car so I decided to put a smile on my face for the family. Everyone was waiting for mom to arrive to make dinner. "Stan...could you help me out here"? "Jeesh Jude it's almost 8:30 where were you we're starving here!" "Oh, I ran over to Chuck and Carol's, they asked me to come over for some pizza after work and then I met Corrie for a little bit. I didn't dare say that Jerry was there and it was a party. Stan just stood there and starred at me. I knew I'd better change the subject or no one would be eating dinner. "Hey look you guys, mom's tired and I already had some pizza, you all eat, I'm not hungry". We all sat together letting the kids talk about their day and had some good laughs. After dinner, Stan came up behind me to kiss me but I shrugged him off. "What's wrong hon"? "Nothing, I just have to clean up". "Sure...I bet if Jerry did that you wouldn't push him away would you"? "What are you talking about?...Jerry's my boss and that's as far as it goes"! "WAS HE THERE TONIGHT...WELL...WAS HE....IS THAT WHY YOU WERE SO LATE"? Stan's voice grew very loud as usual when I ignored his jealous remarks. I tried everything I knew not to erupt but I never did know how to conquer those feelings I had bottled up even before meeting Stan. I never had lost my temper with my first husband, or anyone else for that matter, but Stan stirred me right up to the boiling point. "YES..he was there...with his hand out to comfort me. He was sticking up for you...are you happy now"? "What do you mean by that"? Stan's face dropped as he responded very angrily. "O.K., I called you at work to invite you to join me and they said that you were no longer working there since yesterday; guess you just forgot to tell me about that right?" The look on Stan's face said it all...he had no words left and we decided to just go to separate rooms for a while and cool off.

The next day Corrie came up to me and asked me to grab a bite with me after work. I called home to tell Stan to warm up some leftovers. "Stan, I really won't be home late, Corrie just wants to unload some problems she's having with her boyfriend Art". "Okay be careful...luv ya". "Yeah, me too".

Corrie and I decided to do a few lines of crystal before we ate....it curbs the appetite. Corrie cared a lot for Art but they were having a lot of problems 'cause he was also a drug dealer. "Judy, I want to run over to the bar ...I know that Art's there and I really want to see him". As we were driving I looked at Corrie suddenly....."CORRIE...STOP the car, I want to get out, you go ahead!" "Come on Judy, it will just take a little time"! "Nope, I have to go home, stop here at the phone booth, Stan will pick me up". She looked at me like I lost it but I never felt more strongly about getting out of the truck as I did at that moment. As she pulled away I stood next to the phone booth shaking. I didn't know what was happening...was it the crystal..was I losing it?" Here I was in the middle of nowhere. *Was I hearing a different voice inside me?* I managed to call Stan and it seemed like forever until he arrived. "Hey babe...what's going on"? Stan's smile and hug was real reassuring. I tried to explain it all to him but he just kept staring at me in confusion. "Judy...have you been doing crystal?" "Yeah...so what?...you do weed all the time". "Hon...crystal is a lot more dangerous than pot. The kids have been asking me what's wrong with you lately....they've noticed a change in you. You've been biting their heads off a few times and that's just not like you at all". Stan was right and when I got home I showed him the stash of crystal I had and dumped it down the toilet. Fortunately for me I was only on it for a few months and I had no trouble without it. I had counseled teen's years before and never did any of that junk. What was happening to me? I used to stay far away from evil crap and now it seemed like I was being drawn to it.

"How could I deceive myself like this? Whose voice was I listening to"?

"Judy...Hi!" It was Corrie's and she didn't sound very good on the phone. "Corrie...what's up...what's wrong. you weren't at work; I've been calling you, ..where were you?" "Well...that's because I've been in jail for three days!" "IN JAIL,...WHAT,...WHY?" "Judy you were so smart to get out of the truck when you did. I drove to the bar to meet Art and his friend ran out with a briefcase...told me to hold it for him for a while, threw it in the back of the truck and told me to wait....he would send Art out. I waited for about 25 minutes and no one came out. I got mad and took off but as I drove down the street there was a police blockade....they were everywhere. They pulled me out of the truck, searched my purse, found some Coke and got the briefcase out. I was flat on the ground with loaded guns pointed at me". "Corrie...YOU WERE SET UP....but who"? "Jude...you know what was in the briefcase? Guns, drugs all kind of illegal paraphernalia, I spent 3 days in the Women's Correctional Facility. I'm going to find out just who set me up...better not be Art that's all I have to say!" "CORRIE, CORRIE....listen....I'm at work...I have to hang up...talk to you later!"   When I hung up all I could think about was that I would have been with her and arrested. For once I had made a good decision to get out of her truck and then throw all that crystal down the toilet. This is not what I left my first husband for. I left because I fell in love and wanted a happy life together with Stan....but it's turning out to be a nightmare!

(Stan)

Time had become my enemy. I had much too much of idle time on my hands with no idea what to do with it. The kids, now in their teens, were busy with their own lives. Kurt had taken on a newspaper delivery job and the very first day I found him in the living room with papers all over the place and the TV on. "KURT!....what do you think you are doing?" "Just folding the papers...why?" "WHY? Ummmm....you can't be doing that inside the house....take it all out to the garage where it belongs!" "The garage?" Kurt answered back with a real look of disappointment "YEAH...that's where newspaper work is done...hello?"   He looked really upset. His plans to do the work while being entertained were smashed...but he had a real good attitude and the garage became his permanent newspaper assembly area without any further argument. Holly was busy growing into a beautiful young lady with all of its ups and downs. Boys were beginning to drop by looking for her and Steve had decided to buy his first car. He was a year older than Kurt but both of them would soon be getting their driving licenses at the same time. "Hey Dad I can get a hold of this great '78 Dodge Charger from a friend of mine for $400 but it doesn't have an engine. You and Judy gonna keep that old Dodge or what? "Well Steve, as soon as we get more income coming in, I'll buy a newer car and maybe we can take the engine out of it and transfer it to your Charger, but see if you can have your friend hold on to it for a while O.K?" My answer gave Steve a big smile but I could see the impatience every boy that age has about getting his own wheels.

Here I was out of work once again and this time just hanging around the house still fuming about being fired from May Centers. The more the days came and went, the more angry I became and the more it showed around the kids especially around my wife. She was working every day and couldn't understand my depression. Arguments happened frequently between us. It was like a 'spirit' of agitation and irritability had come between us like rough sandpaper. What had started out years ago as a flaming love affair had become boring and flat. Our intimacy sexually had suffered the most and had caused even more stress between us. What made it worse for me was Judy's continual talk about how great her boss was and how nice he was to her at work. My anger over not working had also taken on a lot of jealousy. One day I found myself walking around the neighborhood in a mental 'fog' wondering what my life was all about but especially why I seemed to always wind up in this position of hopelessness. "HEY STAN!" The voice of a guy I had met once during one of my walks loomed loudly from inside the open garage I had just passed. As I turned around, Dave came running out. "STAN,...I've seen you walking past me some days,...what's up?" "OH...just taking it easy between temp jobs". "REALLY", he responded quickly. "My wife and I have a side business of small pottery things we make in the garage and we sell them to local stores. We're doing pretty good at it too but we need some help to clean them and paint them....interested?" "Hmmm, maybe....but look, you look'n to pay anything for the help?" "Oh yeah sure Stan, we'll pay per piece. Hey look, maybe your kids would like to help too...you know...whenever any of you have some spare time". "Yeah, I could do that...might be fun, I'll be back tomorrow. Dave showed me the garage operation. It looked real creative and at least it would occupy some of my idle hours.

"Hi Stan, what'd you do today anything?" Judy's comment as she walked into the house irritated me to the max but instead of reacting to it violently as I had usually been doing, I told her about the opportunity around the corner in Dave's garage. "Look Judy, temp jobs have all of sudden dropped out of sight. I'm sure there will be something offered soon but in the meantime between me and the kids, if they are interested, it could bring in maybe $80 a day. "What kind of pottery do they make" ""Oh just really cute stuff like frogs, and animals and flowers and stuff". "And they're making good money at that?" "I guess....who cares...Dave said he'd pay me and the kids per piece so....I'm going to go over there tomorrow. "I guess, sounds O.k." I could tell by her voice that she wasn't too impressed but kind of relieved to see me doing something besides just hanging around. After being instructed by Dave as to what he needed for the pottery, I noticed that each and every piece had a small spout attached to it which really had nothing to do with what the pottery design was all about. "Hey Dave, what's the deal with all the small spouts in the pottery...they all look like bongs.....for smoking marijuana; oh yeah......now I see Dave...you are selling bongs...right?" "Right, hey look Stan...whatever I can make a buck on...you smoke grass a little right?" "Sure Dave...hey...I don't care, .it looks like a real clever way to make money".

As days past, I spent a lot of time in Dave's garage and the kids decided to help out but we didn't describe the pottery as smoking bongs to them. Anything but! Judy even decided to join in some nights and a little on the weekends. At least the project provided a little fun for all of us and relaxed our marital situation somewhat. Christmas was fast approaching and I had finally been able to get another temp position. I drove out from the house that first day on the job and the fog was so thick I could hardly see the stop sign a block away. As I began to pull up closer to the corner, two headlights came around the corner from the passenger side of my car and slammed into me. I heard glass breaking and metal crunching and all I could think of was oh damn, this can't be happening again! I got out of the car and met two women who had hit me. They seemed dazed and confused. The front of their car looked really bad but mine seemed only to have minor scratches. It was amazing! Half their grill lay on the ground and I was literally untouched! Suddenly, a woman pushing a baby carriage appeared out of nowhere through the thick fog. It was fairly early and still quite dark but she came right over to me and said...."I saw the whole accident, if you want I'd be happy to be your witness". What the hell, where'd she come from?...this is amazing! Seven o'clock in the morning, thick fog, dim light and a woman with a baby carriage appears out of nowhere as a witness for me? Wow...I must have pleased 'the gods' I thought. Within a week I had a check in my hands for over $400, the amount I settled on with the woman driver's insurance company to repaint the front bumper area of my car. I never did that of course, the money went straight for all the Christmas presents we hadn't been able to purchase.....up to that day!

"Our lives had become a lot more distant, except for a deep desire to re-ignite our love affair. 1981 had finally come to an end thank god...or...some gods...whatever! Although Judy and I were still cockeyed optimists we didn't really have the time or money to relax enough. Being with Den and Jackie some evenings and dancing now and then with Ken and Lin helped but they were all trying to handle their own issues and none of us were really much assistance to each other in that respect. The time had come for Elliot's Bar Mitzvah. I had just started to recoup some lost financial ground but there was no way that Judy and I would miss out on this occasion even though it meant flying by the seat of our pants, so to speak, back east for the occasion. I felt real bad for Elliot. Only three years earlier, I had provided his brother Steve with a spectacular Disco Mitzvah party and now I was barely able to fly back and just be in attendance. My former wife was rather frugal and not very good at being original so her best answer to the day was a small reception at her mother's house and a night at the roller-skating rink with Elliot's fiends and some family. It was very uncomfortable for us to be in my former mother-in-law's home and although we understood the tension between us we couldn't wait to get out of there. Steve had flown back east with us of course but as we landed back in San Diego, we finally breathed a big sigh of relief. The entire trip had been filled to overflowing with apprehension and tension, but it was over and only the memory of my youngest son reciting his Hebrew without fault would remain the best part of the trip.

"HeyJude", ….talking and walking around the blocks where we lived as we often did to try to clear the air…..

"You know, it seems like Dennis and Ken have really gotten a lot friendlier lately...have you noticed that? "Hmm, yes I have....guess that's a good thing huh?" "Well, maybe so but remember how Dennis was so adamant not to be friends with Ken? "Yeah, so what? That was then...now is now!" "It's not that babe; I just feel I'm being squeezed out!" "Squeezed out? What'd ya mean by that?" "Oh I don't know...when I'm with them, they just have a great time and I'm kind of ignored". "You know Stan, you are getting more and more critical and finding fault over the stupidest things....do you know that? "Well thanks a lot for understanding....see if I care about your feelings if you ever want to be open with me! "WHAT the heck, let's turn around and go home, I really don't want to argue with you here on the street again!" "Sure, bet you don't act this way with your wonderful boss Jerry!" "Jerry has nothing to do with anything ....what IS your problem anyway?" "How 'bout good sex lady?" "Yeah..how 'bout it Stan?"

I watched angrily as she walked quickly away from me towards home. What the hell is wrong with her anyway I thought.....or me for that matter....
I can't stand living like this much longer!
Have we come all this way just to wind up divorced?

166

I N T E R M I S I O N

(Stan & Judy)

"Take a break from reading for a minute"
You know babe, the readers need a 'time out' from all the craziness they've been reading about so far....and so do we! It's been hard bringing it all back to memory...as a matter of fact, I don't really want to remember it much. The thing is it is so easy now to see the stupid choices we made back then and how deceived we were by the voices we followed within us. You got that right Stan, sometimes when I'm writing about different situations, I have to catch my breath. I almost want to cry but then there were some fun times so I get to laugh some too.....it was like being on a rollercoaster ride and not being able to get off! Remember what you said your mom always told you? What was that Jude? She said "when there's no money....love flies out the window!" Boy is that the truth Jude and it almost did just that several times and we almost got divorced at one point because of all the stress and lack huh? Mmmmm, yeah Stan, but our love has lasted and grown deeper. I just can't believe we let ourselves be so suckered in by 'so called' psychics, witchcraft and new age garbage. Our curiosity almost killed us....actually it almost killed you for real!

Ouch! Did you have to remind me about that? You know Jude, I know it's hard for most people to believe that there really is a reality to the spiritual world but it's not what they think it is. I hope that by the end of the story they will be able to discern just whose voice it is that they are hearing and making their choices from. Oh

I know they will Stan. O.K, I think I've been able to refresh and re-energize enough. **Hey you...reading this page...yes you!** Why not stop and do the same? This is not just a story of our lives over a definite period of time. It is meant to be an awakening to why you're at where you're at. You know, wherever we are, it's all due to the choices we made, are making and will ever make.

(Stan, continued)

Oh well, another new year....another new temp to fulltime job opened up. Here I go again...what's new? I was once again in a small company needing some technical illustration supervision, which actually was somewhat strange due to my limited knowledge but, the department consisted only of me and Terri. She was a gal who had been there a few years and seemed quite upset that she wasn't offered the job instead of an outsider like me. So, the atmosphere between us wasn't exactly the best but as time went on, we managed to join creative forces and worked quite easily together. 'Together' was a word which was to take on a whole new meaning as the months came and went. I got tired of driving Steven's Dodge Charger, which we had managed to power up with the engine from our old Dodge that had been hit at the mall the previous year. Finances were flowing in once more and I decided to buy a second car. I really wanted a Lincoln or Caddy but I wound up with a 1979 Olds 98 Regency with a Diesel engine. When it was new, it was called the car with a $20,000 'knock'....cause that's what it cost new and sounded like when it started up. It had two 25gal additional fuel tanks installed in the trunk and could go over 1,000 miles without refueling and...it was really nice looking and had a very luxurious interior along with pretty low mileage. Anyway, it was mine: Judy had the smaller Ford and Steve was freed up to putter in and around in the Charger until he got his license.

Terri was living with Rick, her 'significant other', and Judy and I got fairly friendly with the two of them, enough so to be invited

168

one day to join them at a motorcycle 'wet-tee-shirt' party held way out in the country in the woods. Judy and I looked somewhat obvious driving into the area in our Olds 98. Judy had to show a little cleavage for us to be admitted but it seemed to be all in fun so we arrived and the folks there were just having a good time with roasted pig in a blanket and a lot of booze and drugs floating around. Terri's boyfriend was very jealous of my relationship with her just like my jealousy with Judy's boss Jerry. "Hey man", yelled one of the guys standing next to Rick "Have a hit on this, it's really good weed". I had no trouble accepting the marijuana.....that is...what I thought was marijuana. Within a real short time I was staggering all over the place and found myself completely immobilized face down in the dirt between two cars. JUDY...HELP! I could hear her voice and Terri's voice near me but I could not move my body. What was more frightening was that I couldn't feel my body at all....and they couldn't hear my silent scream.....I was paralyzed but my brain was wide awake. **I was terrified….I had no connection with my body!**

WHAT IF MY HEART STOPPED?

(Judy)

WOW what a party and what an entrance, I felt a little intimidated lifting my shirt and me being braless but what an exciting adventure. As Stan and I spotted Terri and Rick, Stan headed right over to Terri, jealousy got me right to my stomach but I kept it to myself. Marijuana was everywhere and I knew that Stan would be in his glory. I watched as Stan grabbed a joint from Rick's friend. "Come on Jude, take a hit!" "No, you know I hate the feeling I get with that stuff". "Yeah, I know, you get real quiet which isn't such a bad thing". I heard the laughter from Terri and felt that jealousy in the pit of my stomach rising up again. Stan loved to smoke the stuff and so did she.

"STAN!...are you all right...what's wrong?" I watched as Stan dropped the weed and staggered toward our car. Terri and I looked at each other with amazement as he fell to the ground and lay flat on his face. I heard him whisper, "Just let me lie here for a while". I felt full of anger, here I am at this wild motorcycle party in the woods all alone and my husband is passed out from smoking some marijuana. I thought it was kind of strange though 'cause Stan had never reacted like that before but I was still very angry about the whole situation. *Oh well, may as well have some beer and join in the fun, I thought!* Guys were playing their guitars, some people were singing along with them and some gals were in the back of pickup truck being sprayed with water on their tee shirts. There were a lot of single men who began hitting on me but here I was a married woman with a passed out husband on the ground. I began flirting a little but in the back of my mind wondering about my passed out husband. I broke away from the crowd to check up on him and found him motionless in the same spot. "STAN!...what's wrong? Get up!" Fear started to grab me as I ran to get Terri. "Terri, help me...Stan has been lying there for over an hour...what was in that weed he smoked...was it laced with something?" "Judy, I don't know". "Terri go and ask Rick what this is all about, I'm scared, I can't get Stan up! The next thing I knew, Terri was on the ground lying next to Stan talking to him. After a while she got him to respond and by now I figured that he was O.K....he just needed Terri's voice. I felt a rage of anger and took off to mingle in the crowd again. What the hell kind of hold does this woman have on my husband? I looked back and saw Stan on his knees and then slowly getting up and walking still looking very dazed! "Rick! What in the world did you give Stan? What was in that weed you gave him to knock him out like that?" Rick just looked at me and laughed. *Is he jealous of Stan around Terri?* As Stan came near me he just grabbed me and apologized. "Judy, I can't explain what happened but I was never so frightened in my life! I could hear every word you were saying but I just couldn't respond! I know it sounds crazy but I think that weed I smoked was laced with something...I couldn't move any part of my body, I felt totally paralyzed...like I was tranquilized or something! I don't understand...I'm no pot-head.. .I mean...I don't hang out all day smok'n weed....or am I just rationalizing....I feel so dumb." *I felt the anger beginning to leave and I felt real sorry for my husband.* "I just didn't understand. I was angry that you smoked and left me all alone here for over two hours". I could see Stan staring at Rick just wondering what was in that joint....it looked like Stan was about to start a fight with Rick.

"Hey Jude, I feel real slimy around here...let's go...we don't belong with this crowd of bikers. We shouldn't have come here in the first place!" On the way home all I could think about was how fortunate that my Stan didn't die. I hated weed and the addiction and hold it had on my husband. "Stan, I hate drugs, it changes us". "Oh Jude it's a tension breaker and helps relax me that's all". "Relax?....you mean almost kill you...don't you?" "Hon that stuff Rick gave me was definitely laced no one passes out for 2 hours from weed. I couldn't get any info from Rick. All I know is that I walked into the party area, he handed me the joint and the next thing I knew I'm paralyzed on the ground but my brain was wide awake sober. No one gets that way from smokin' a little weed!" "Well Terri brought you back to life my dear by lying next to you". "Really Jude honey, I don't remember that"." "Well that's when your brain connected with your body...she sure has a way with you!" "Yeah but at least I got up and when I did there you were laughing and drinking with a total stranger!" "So...what else was I supposed to do, you and your pot were passed out for over two hours.....I can't believe you're saying that...what was I supposed to do...lay on the ground beside you for two hours in the dirt?" "Who knows, no one else reacted that way did they?" Stan and I never really knew the whole story. I just hoped it would be a wakeup call for him and he's stop smokin' the stuff.

"Hey Jude...who was at the door?" "It was the Landlord; he gave us notice to move. His parents are moving back to town and they need to fix up the inside of the house for them". "Hey, you know... Kurt said that one of his customers from his paper route is moving". "So?" "Well Kurt said that the owner wants to rent it. It's in the same area but a lot nicer than here and it's a lot larger. The rent's a little higher but we can afford it...and besides it's even closer to the kid's school. He likes Kurt and want's to rent it to people he knows, so what do you think?" "What do I think?...let's do it...sounds good to me!" The boys were in high school and Holly was in middle school. Kurt was very involved with choir and very popular and Holly was a Pop Warner cheerleader. We loved going to the football games nearby. Steve was becoming a good mechanic and loved working on his car. It seemed at last that things were turning for the best. I loved my job at the nursery and tried real hard not to talk about Jerry too much in front of Stan. Jerry asked me to work some extra hours so because there weren't enough employees and me being a workaholic I volunteered. Stan became suspicious and I noticed that he was staying later at work. The newness of our new home wore off and we began fighting again. He was still jealous of Jerry, no matter what I said and I was the same about Terri. One night I came home late and left the dinner in the oven for everyone.....our schedules were getting real crazy. The phone rang and I hoped it would be Stan. "Hi...Judy...this is Terri". My stomach dropped. "Hi Terri...what's up?" "I just wanted you to know that Stan's on his way home, we had to work late. Is there any way you and I can meet for a drink tomorrow night?" I was stunned. "Well...okay...where?" We set up a time near a Bar & Grill near her work. I was very confused and didn't understand what was happening but I sure was curious and couldn't wait for the meeting to happen. Everyone got home just then and we finally were able to sit down together. We always had fun as a family, telling jokes and catching up on the day's events.

After dinner I mentioned my meeting with Terri to Stan. His comment was..."Oh..that's nice!" His remark sounded strange but I decided to let it go at that. The next day came fast and I hurried through my work and drove to Kearny Mesa about 30 minutes away and met Terri. She was already there so I ordered a drink with her to be sociable and to settle my nerves. We actually got along O.K., even had a few laughs then the bomb hit. "Judy, I met you here for a reason". "I figured as much...what's up?" "Well

Stan and I have been working pretty closely together for some time now and we really enjoy the time together. I understand that the two of you haven't been getting along. Stan says you are always fighting...sex is lousy and you've lost interest in each other"." **So what are you saying?**" "What I'm saying is that your husband and I have spent a lot of hours together". "**STOP!**...ARE YOU HAVING AN AFFAIR WITH STAN?" "No...he only kissed me, we were sitting in the car talking and he leaned over and kissed me". "I can't believe you're telling me this Terri, I guess I really do have a reason to be jealous". "Look Judy, if you don't want your husband, I'm just warning you...I DO!" "OVER MY DEAD BODY YOU BITCH!...you come near my husband again and I'll rip your eyes out!" I stormed out of the bar and sped off. I was in shock. All kinds of thoughts rushed through my head and I realized that I could really lose Stan. What kind of game are we both playing? I pulled the car over to the side of the road and just broke, I couldn't stop crying. Oh my God...what has happened to our marriage? I felt so out of control. It was as if some strange 'force' was trying to come between us and separate what we had both worked so hard for. We had come to California to run away from that crazy spiritual world and now I'm finding we were hitting another.....this one was a wall of division! *Oh God...please help us!* As I pulled into our driveway I felt numb. I knew I had to fight for my husband but I didn't know how. It seemed like forever getting out of the car to face Stan...but what would I say? He heard me pull up and was waiting by the door. We just stood there for a moment and looked at each other. I burst out in tears. Stan had such compassion and we just held each other and spent the next few hours talking. We loved each other and I knew that Terri was a huge warning. She represented excitement as Jerry did for me. We had both lost that in each other and wanted to capture it again through someone who showed interest. *Where do we go from here?*

(Stan)

"Judy, I can't believe Kenny!" "Why Stan. what's wrong?" "You know what I've been trying to tell you for months now, that he and

Denny have become best buddies? I'm really happy for Ken that they're getting along but I'm kind of a third wheel now. Remember when Den met Ken back east and he told me never to bring Ken to his house? I tried everything to get them together and now I'm out of the picture! Remember the night we all went to that outdoor meeting that Ken & Lin brought us to? "What meeting Stan?" You know, the one with Terry Cole-Whittaker... the New Age Prosperity High Priestess? "Oh yeah, she drove up in her Limo and Mink Coat...sooo?" Well, he was really into it but I wasn't too happy about our friendship then and I think he knew it bigtime! "Oh come on Stan, it's not that bad, you're just feelin' down about yourself that's all". "Well maybe so but you know the food label I designed for the new sauce he's trying to sell?" "Oh yeah hon it looked really good what's the problem?" "Problem? I'll tell you what problem! I designed it for him and he said he'd pay me $200 someday...and I would have waited no matter how long but he just went out and bought some new exercise equipment for himself...what a slap in the face huh? Ya think he would've given me at least fifty bucks...or something! I got really pissed and told him off. He got really mad at me too. "I guess that ends our friendship with all of them right?" "Hey, if Den wants to side with Ken then that's way it has to be for a while. We have other friends to be with, I don't really care anymore! By the way babe, I quit my job and don't get upset; I'm already hired on at a new temp assignment with another client". "You quit? You really quit? How come? "Well, I went to my boss and told her that Terri and I were working too closely together and getting too familiar. I suggested that she should let one of us go. Since Terri was there a lot longer than me, I was the one that had to leave". "Stan, you did that for me?" "Yeah but I did that more for us. I want us to get back to our love affair; we've come too far to let it all go. You know, as beautiful as it is here in San Diego, everything seems very 'plastic' somehow...like dreamland...sur-realistic! Were we deceived by even coming here?" "I don't know Stan, I've never really liked it here but the weather is great and you loved it a lot since we arrived...what are you saying?" "Nothin' really, just feel this total 'spirit' of confusion on me all the time and look how close we've come to even thinking about divorce; there's got to be something more real in life than just existing isn't there?" "Maybe we should find a Church or something" "CHURCH? ....are you serious?. I'm Jewish remember?" "Oh Jewish!...c'mon Stan....so what...maybe a minister can explain everything to us". "Forget it Jude, I don't believe that there's a real God, but I do believe that those spirits are real we left back east....maybe we should find a real good Clair Voyant here, you know, like a Tarot Card reader?" "I don't know anymore luvies, I feel like we're trying to **reach through a veil**....it just gets heavier and heavier....whatever you say, we definitely have to find an answer. Thank God our children are all healthy and doing O.k. or I'd really be a basket case by now". "There you go again thanking God ...why do we quote something or someone we don't even believe in?" "You know something sweetheart; I can't handle much more of this conversation ...my head's starting to hurt, let's just see what happens O.k.?"

"SAN", it was Jackie's voice on the phone. "Remember when I got Raelyn over to your house to help you find out about those 'spirits' you always talked about? She described your father and an old green car with yellow rims when you were a little boy! Did you ever get to go to that church to meet the minister she told you about? She's here with me and wants to know what happened". "Yeah Jack, we went to see the minister but all he could tell us was to come to the church and start getting into the Bible". "Well? What happened?" "WHAT happened? I'll tell you what happened...Jude and I ran out of there as fast as we could.....I ain't gonna get involved with any church that's for sure! Besides...nothing personal (and don't tell Raelyn) but I think her elevator doesn't go quite to the top...in fact I don't think she has an elevator! You know, she said a lady in white clothing approached her on a bus and told her she wouldn't live past 40yrs old!" "Stop SAN! ...you got me laughing and she's coming back from the bathroom...I gotta hang up now" "Was that Jackie on the phone?" "Hmmm...yup...it was!" "Well...what did she want?" "Oh, she was with Raelyn...you know the gal who said she was a 'clair voyant'. She was just interested if we had ever followed her advice. I told her what happened at the church that's all". "I remember Raelyn and that meeting....what a letdown". "O.K. then let's drive down and take a walk through Balboa Park, I love that place, it's such a pretty day".

(Judy)

It was nearing the Holidays and Christmas was my favorite time of the year. I loved all of the decorations and music. As we walked through the park I felt this draw toward a Psychic sitting at her table outside. "Hey Stan, let's stop at the psychic and find out what's in our future!" As we walked toward her we both stopped in our tracks. "You know Stan, all of a sudden I'm uncomfortable about this ...how 'bout you?" "Yeah Jude, she looks a little weird with that funny turban around her head. Remember the last time we went to a psychic back home and everyone in the office went?" "I don't want to remember" "O.K. .forget it then!"

We had a great Christmas. We had a beautiful tree which we also called a Hanukah Bush for Stan and Steven's Jewish holiday celebration. My dad also flew out from Florida and that made it really special. He was such a character. He was tall, bowlegged and dressed really funny in striped shirts, checkered pants and fisherman's hat or sometimes a cowboy hat....but he always made us laugh with so many jokes ....we could never understand how he remembered them all. 1984 came and it was a fun year. Our two boys Kurt and Steve were graduating from High School. They were such good kids. We never had to worry much about either of them. Stan's ex wife Joyce and my ex husband Joe arrived for the graduation. There was a time years ago that we thought they should date each other but realized that would never work even though they had a lot in common. It was good to see them together and have all of us witness our sons get their diplomas. Kurt and Steve had decided to go to Grossmont Junior College in the next town for a few years until they could decide on their careers. Steve was real good mechanically with his hands and Kurt was a wiz at computers. Stan and I and our ex mates decided to go out to dinner and dancing after the graduation celebration. It felt weird but turned out to be a lot of fun. We even got to dance with our ex's. By then work was getting quite stressful. The Nursery was beginning to go through financial problems and was considering bankruptcy. Chuck and Jerry were always behind closed doors. They introduced me to Mike.... a man from San Francisco, he was a big man and very intelligent. I had no idea what was going on but a lot of major decisions were going on behind those closed doors.

The summer months were flying by and Stan and I were feeling the pressure between us again. We were estranged from Ken and Linda and now also Jackie and Dennis. Money had become an issue and had led to a lot of arguments and fights. My brother Michael was getting married in Georgia so I decided this would be a good time to take a break from all the strife and fly out for the occasion. My mom paid for my flight and it couldn't have come a better time. As I was packing for the trip, Holly, now at that difficult age of 15, came in and introduced me to her new boyfriend Lee. He didn't seem to have too many manners but I brushed it off to immaturity. I started to feel uneasy as I watched his roving hands on my daughter but little did I realize what he was really like. *Of all times*, I thought, *just when I'm leaving for five days!* Oh well, whatever, it felt good to be getting away from Stan for a while. I wasn't sorry to leave and I really didn't miss him.

I had another problem to contend with when I arrived for the wedding. My stepfather Mike, my mother's second husband, Michael's father, was there. Mom ran away from this man when I was 16. I really hated him then for all the cruel things he did to me as a kid growing up....especially putting me in a dark cellar when I didn't eat my dinner. When I first saw him again I felt very squeamish remembering all the nutty things he did to me. I thought he was a crazy man! I decided though, that I would find out more about who this man had become throughout the years and I felt sadness for him. He was a lonely man and I became a lot more compassionate. We talked for quite a while which helped ease the burden I had carried for so many years. The wedding was really different; more like the Hippy Generation of the late 60's and early 70's. I was just happy for my brother. It was his first marriage and he would become an instant father of 2 children from his new bride. I stayed for a few days longer than planned and finally decided to call home. I felt so peaceful away from all the problems at home that somehow I didn't miss Stan At all....which really frightened me!

"Stan, how are you?" "I miss you green eyes, when are you coming home?" *I couldn't say I missed him at all.* "I'll be back tomorrow. How are the kids?" "Kurt's always busy with his paper route; Steve's always tinkering around his car and Holly's almost always at her friend's house. Haven't seen them very much...you know, I've got a lot of projects to complete in my garage studio for that new design client of mine...there's a absolute deadline to finish". "Is Holly with that boy Lee?" "I guess so". "What do you mean I guess so? Haven't you been keeping a eye on her?" "Listen Jude, she's always staying the night with her friends. If you were so worried about her you should have stayed home!" I felt real frustration and anger arising and tried to push it down. There was so much I wanted to say like...can't you do just a little thing like watch the kids and take them out for dinner or movies just to spend some time with them? Stan always wanted me to do everything for the children. I had to admit, it was a little difficult for Stan as far as Holly was concerned. She always felt that he wasn't her real dad and never would allow herself to get close with him even though he tried many times over the years. She always pushed him away. "Stan, I'll see you tomorrow, It's flight 707, arrives at 6:37pm". "I love you babe". "See ya then Stan". As I hung up the phone my heart ached. I had a hard time telling Stan I loved him. We've been through so much. I hated to leave my brother and mom and head back west to who knows what! As the plane landed I felt sick to my stomach. I had to face all the drama and problems again but I never realized just how many problems lay ahead.

(Stan)

"Hey Jude, stop writing....I think our readers need a break from all the details of the next few years. How 'bout just giving them an overview....you know...like a time crunch...whatever!" "Hmmmm, I think you're right Stan, somehow we managed to stay away from all the 'spirit stuff' with the exception of our daughter going through bad years but nothing of any other major interference in our lives happened" "Well except for our involvement with the theatre group and how that producer who was a so-called 'witch' prayed over one of the plays for success?" "Boy do I....and she won an award too,,,,but her husband almost walked through a glass door! .I told her to get the friggen candles off the stage and stop the chanting. Boy, did she get mad at me." "Yeah Stan, and you were the only one who didn't get an award for that play remember that?" "Guess I've never forgot huh!"

S Y N O P S I S

(Judy)

Okay babe I don't want to bore whoever is reading this story. I'll just hit on the highlights and then the meat of our deep problem and our attempts to **"reach through the veil of deceit"** which continues to cause confusion and division, and has now struck our daughter. Holly turned 15 and her encounter with a new boyfriend was disastrous. I lost her for the next couple of years. She became a totally different person. Straight A's to barely passing grades, skipping school, hanging with a bad crowd of teenagers. It was hard on the family to watch as she slipped away from all of us. When I met this boy I got an eerie feeling about him. The next few years were a living hell but with a lot of love and perseverance I got our Holly back and today she's a beautiful young lady and a mother of two beautiful children. During this time, Stan and I had also decided to join a community theater group. We loved people and live stage performances. I had never worked in theatre but Stan had been involved in Stage design and construction and I was persuaded to produce one of the plays. I had no idea as to how to go about it but I had plenty of help. I really got into the roll and had a lot of fun We were involved with several different plays over the next three years and at the end of the last year when they called my name for best Producer, I was shocked. I was so proud as I received a trophy. I had never had the courage to do anything like that before. I still give you credit hon for always believing in me. Boy do I ever remember that woman "high priestess" lighting candles the day of the play and chanting her rituals for success.

You caught her and told her to stop but she wouldn't. It was "The Philadelphia Story" performed in a retirement center, wasn't it? Stan, you did a spectacular set design and everyone got an award except you! She sure got our curiosity going again about all that "spirit" crap! We also did a stage production on a normal stage that was all about Noah and the Ark. When Noah's wife agreed to allow two of her sons to switch wives in that performance a whole bunch of folks got up and walked out.....we thought that was really strange but....oh well...couldn't please everyone we thought! Most of our memories were a lot of fun but it was very time consuming, much less sitting through virtually every performance of literally every play so we finally withdrew from further involvement. Oh yeah, then our landlord put our house up for sale and offered us the option of buying it but after bringing in an expert who knew about a 'balloon payment' involved with the purchase; we decided to just find another home to rent in the same school district. Our boys had graduated but Holly had one more year and...what a year it was! Wow! We were in the largest home we had ever rented. Holly graduated with good grades and Stan, you were working full time for a very large Defense Contractor. I was working for a large Bank....money was rolling in and everything seemed to be turning around for us. The time came to move again but the boys were going to Junior College and had moved out on their own, Steve with a friend in an apartment and Kurt joined a Church where he lived with a group of other guys. We found a great ground floor apartment with a pool, Jacuzzi, racket ball court and tennis courts closer in to San Diego. Hmmm, you were kind of excited Stan but I cried a lot missing the boys and all the excitement and although Holly moved in with us for a while she also moved out within a year with some friends near the beach. So here we were with what is known by everyone as "empty nesters".

"You know something babe, as I reflect back on that final move, remember when my Vanity plates were stolen just before my bankruptcy back east and I never saw them again?" "Uh...kinda..why?" "Well as we were packing up the house before our move to the new apartment, one of the plates appeared in a box!" "Oh yeah.. I remember that...are you sure about that whole plate thing?" "SURE?...absolutely!....I never saw them again until that move! In fact, when the plates were stolen, they had 1973 registration tabs on them. The plate that popped up in the box had a 1974 tab on it and I had never had the chance to re-register the plates for that year! It really freaked me out and I still can't figure it all out. " "Hmmm...yeah...sure.....maybe!"

False Hopes

Chapter 10

FALSE HOPES

(Stan)

Boy Hon, you sure did a good job of synopsizing! "Synopsizing?"...what kind of word is that?" I dunno, I made it up! "O.K., O.K., word-man, let's get back to the story. Remember that guy Dave and his wife Brenda at your workplace? They invited us up to their home in Alpine to meet a "Psychic" friend of theirs?" I sure do crab-eyes, that day was the beginning of the end for us huh?...or should I say the beginning of the beginning? "You lost me man-of–words....all I know is that her name was Judy, like mine, and she pulled out those cards....what were they called?" Tarot Cards Jude! "Oh yeah, Tarot Cards...she looked straight at us and said that we had raised the dead. I think my face turned blue or something you know?

DECEIVED AGAIN
"Hey you guys, I conduct a course in my house every week and I only charge $25 a session. Why don't you start attending, maybe you can start to understand why all that stuff back east happened to you....and you'll find out what's in store in the future too so you can control your lives once and for all!" **(Judy the Psychic)**

That was the "HOOK" wasn't it Jude? "It sure was. You'd think that with all we were involved with over the years we wouldn't have gotten involved. What were we thinking? We were such gluttons for punishment and still so naïve to those deceiving spirits! All those worthless meetings at her apartment and then in the little cottage she bought with all the bucks she swiped from us and the rest of her dumb clients....but you know Stan, she was absolutely sure of her **'spirit friends'**....and we were all real eager to find out as much as we could". How 'bout that session when she started to call out our **"spirit guides"**....Mine was an artist. Yours was a guy named Brad who stabbed someone and had come back to do it right! You used to run around the house after that meeting pretending you were like the guy in the movie Psycho!! Remember there were about 6 or 7 of us present that day?

Judy (the psychic) cried out in amazement to one of the women...."Oh my, you are very special....your spirit guide is Jesus!" We were all in awe over her statement and wondered how that gal had Jesus as her very own "spirit guide" "Yeah but we felt like we were on the bottom of the barrel compared to her" JUDE! That wasn't the worst of it! "What do you mean Stan?" Well, we got Holly involved with us eventually and Judy tried to put us all through time 'regression'. We started to do that a little but fortunately Holly could not and it all stopped. We even got Kurt to come once....what were we thinking anyway...the whole experience was bizarre. He just sang you that song called *"Wind beneath My Wings"* then laughed at the session he was at. "You think THAT was bizarre? How about when she said we needed to have a "deliverance" from all the evil spirits we had brought with us?" Who could forget that scene? You borrowed $3,500 for us and then I caught you lying on the bed in our apartment the night that the 'supposed' deliverance was going to take place with white clothes on so you'd be "pure enough" to receive the "Exorcism". I laughed so hard I couldn't believe you! "Well, when we saw Judy a few days later, she looked like she'd been through a war all right!.....her eyes were blackened, she looked terrible... and she told us we were one of the most difficult exorcisms she had ever done. But, we felt light as a feather for days afterwards huh? Yeah, I guess, but it sure didn't last long. We kept at it though with her and one night while asleep I experienced what she called a **"Pre-Cognition"**...you know...where I was literally in the future and witnessed a helicopter exploding! I even recognized the water below as the San Francisco Bay and there really was a helicopter crash! I woke up yelling and scared you! Scared me?..It sure did, it scared me out of my wits. And then I went to see her at her little cottage a week later and found an empty lot. Right between two other houses, her's had been totally removed!

No house...No Judy the Psychic! Hello?

"You know Stan; so many things happened in just a few years, we could have written this book just about those years alone. I sure had several great jobs. I worked for an electrical firm that hadn't paid its taxes and the IRS closed their doors. One day I went to work and found the notice on the door with no paycheck! Then a pager company and then a Temp job at the bank that turned into a permanent position which I loved". Yeah, I know and remember how one of the dozen Tech Illustrators I was in charge of at that Defense Contractor I worked for kept putting Jesus "Tracts" on all of the work he turned in every day? He was just one of a bunch of Christians there who were determined to convert me! I told him one day that if I saw one more tract on the work he turned in, I'd have him fired. "Well? What happened Stan, I kind of remember you telling me about it?" What happened? Nothing! He came back to my desk an hour later with another tract and just laughed as he walked away! "SO...did you fire him?" Naahh, I liked him too much, pretended to just ignore the whole thing. Hey, by then I had even become friends again with Ken and Denny. If I wasn't bombarded at work then Ken was always on my butt about God. Remember the weekend party at Den's house? We were really sacked out around the pool Sunday morning and low and behold Ken showed up, bible in hand with Lin and the boys. I couldn't believe my eyes but he sure left an impression on me! We were also involved at that time with an Herbal product and I was not feeling very good then either. Somehow it had a negative effect on me and I started to get very sick from it but even the doctors couldn't figure out what was wrong. When my head was clear, my body wanted to sleep, when my body felt O.K. my brain wanted to sleep. I was losing a lot of weight and getting very dehydrated. One of the doctors even thought I might have AIDS which really scared me.

(Judy)

Boy, I sure do remember that Hon...and I don't know what came over me; I had no sympathy for you at all. You came to my work one day almost in tears and I turned away from you. It was as if I was being controlled by something.....I had absolutely no emotions, it was a very weird time huh?...I still want that memory to go away!" Well, it went on for about 6 months but all the symptoms suddenly disappeared just as it had started..... like waking up from a nightmare! But I still have aches in my heart over it. I watched you walk down the stairs in tears crying out for my love. You were hurting so bad and I just couldn't give it to you. I felt cold and empty!. We were planning a trip back east to see Elliot graduate from High School and we thought we'd have to cancel the trip because you couldn't sit for that many hours in the plane. You just felt terrible. I remember we had you sitting on a pillow from the soreness and you had a real hard time holding down any food. We tried so hard to meet your family and our friends and have some fun but you got so tired so easily. It was a hard trip but we managed somehow and flew from there to San Francisco to my nephew's wedding. We couldn't find a decent hotel and we wound up in a real flee-bag motel...remember that? "Remember? How could ever forget that place! It looked like roaches wouldn't even stay there and the neighborhood looked pretty scrungy too. We hadn't eaten much that day and for the first time in months we walked across the street into that ugly ethnic grocery store and I bought a bunch of junk food and said... *"If I'm checking out of this world soon then I'm going out happy"*. Yeah Stan and you felt O.K. and from that night on you started getting better. You even ate all that hot Mexican food at the reception with no problem! "Judy, I'm not a praying man, don't believe in this 'Godly thing' BUT....well...I know there were people praying for me at work and Ken and Linda too...and your brother Bob had people praying for me also.....maybe there's something to all this?" Well Stan, Whatever, I'm just glad you got better. It took you a while to gain the weight back. You went down to 148 lbs, you scared me...you didn't look so good, and they never found out what it was did they? "No, the docs gave up I guess...but boy, I had a great time eating 4 and 5 meals a day!"

My heart felt so sad years later the way I treated you then when you were so sick. I had a lot of resentment and anger bottled up during the course of our lives together. After having the beautiful love affair we experienced with each other, going through all of this deception and hard times in our relationship was no fun. Remember that old expression...*'Stop the car, I want to get out'*....that was me. There were so many things going on during this time Stan but of all the incidents that bothered me the most was when you were so sick and we met that lady 'Seton' .....Remember you always slipped and called her **Satan!** "Yeah, I remember her how did we meet her Jude?" Oh, it all started though our friend Barbara who we met at a marketing event with some multi-level product we were involved with. She tried to sell our son Kurt on the stuff but he wasn't interested and told her to talk to us. *"My parents are always into new things" he told her.* Yep Stan, she came over to our apartment and we got involved with it and then we went to a meeting with her and you won the door prize which was a free consultation with Seton. She was some kind of marketing guru. "Oh she sure was a kook! We went through a few months of hell with her didn't we? Great 'door prize' huh? I was not interested at all but Jude you were all for it so you and Barbara went to see her together". The time that freaked me out the most Stan was that Sunday conference she had had on regression. All the lights were turned off in this big hall and we were all told to bring our pillows and to lie down and meditate. You and Holly were together and I was on the other side of the room. I was so afraid. You and Holly were joking about it and thought it was just freaky but I took it seriously. There was a point when she had us yell out the things we hated most about our mother and then our father. Mom was easy for me (at that time) but not my dad. He was my idol. I felt my body freezing up and unable to move at all. My lips were frozen, my heart raced, I thought I was having a heart attack! As she walked around the room she spotted me frozen with tears running down my cheeks. The next thing I knew she was pounding on my chest to release the fear. My mouth was so frozen from fear nothing would come out. Finally I yelled and came back to moving my body. I kept yelling to her... **"what happened to me"?**

"What exactly did happen to you babe"? Oh, she just explained that our minds didn't want to remember things so we shut down. I didn't like her answer, not when it came to my dad, there was no hatred, he was the joy that kept me going in my life. I looked over at you and Holly and you were laughing, never knowing what I experienced because the lights were out. Not a good memory for me, that's for sure. "Boy Jude, we got engulfed in a lot of "New Age" crap huh? It's all over this southern California area. Stan, remember how you had all those meetings with Seton to help you line up with the Universe so you could prosper financially and you could never seem to line yourself up the way she said and that's why things weren't working out for us? My God, we were searching everywhere through everyone to find out what was wrong. We worked so hard at everything we did but nothing ever seemed to work right. You were so frustrated and that lining-up thing was the last straw! Stan, how about when I used to go out to the pool area every weekend and write that book you named "Frenchtown Lady". I used to put my spirit guides on my shoulder, as I used to say, and write and write. Everyone at the pool couldn't wait until I was done. You never could understand how I could remember so many incidents so clearly and word for word conversations. It was pretty good if I must say so. I wrote and you typed and edited.

"Yeah Jude, I couldn't believe you wrote so many personal details, it was like being back in time. Then one day you came in and said that you had 'writer's block', put it down and never finished it. Well, we're nearing the end of this book and the readers will understand all of the 'WHYS' right hon?"

You know the strangest time of our lives? "Ummm...where would I begin Stan the man?" Well, for one thing, I never told you that over the last year I had written away for information about the Baha'i faith, Rosicrucians and a few other mystical and metaphysical beliefs. I can't even remember all of them but a lot of days that I drove up and waited for you to leave work, I tuned into a few Christian stations too but I'd turn it off quick when I saw you coming towards the car! "You're kidding? Christian stations too?" Sure...I don't know even what I was listening to but it felt reassuring somehow. "Hmmmm....gotta confess something babe.....I was tuning in to some of those stations myself sometimes"

Chapter 11

THE UNVEILING

"That which I feared the most had come upon me once again"

(Stan)

Although I was the supervisor of a dozen or so technical illustrators, solidly sure of my full time employment and secure income at the large Defense Contractor, the times had moved the company into a new age of computerized formats and my entire division was wiped out. I had always thought that as head man of the department and as a guy who had streamlined the flow of work to the point of cost cutting and major savings, that I would be the last to be let go or, at the very least, be transferred to another department. However, my total lack of knowledge in the new system found me ousted with everyone else!

"You know Jude, (*I said with a combination of defeat and optimism in my voice*), I have so had it with working for other people, always giving 110% of myself in everything I do and then winding up with nothing. I got a pretty decent severance pay and I can also collect unemployment; I'm going to just get into my own graphics design business and see what happens". The look on my wife's face said it all. She, like myself, couldn't deal with the financial rollercoaster ride anymore. What difference would it make? Inside us were a raging array of emotions and a quiet surrender to the circumstances we continually found ourselves in. Barbara, the gal that sold us on getting into the health drink multi-level business, kept on us a lot and over the next year I saw a need to develop advertising materials for the company. So, I put together a bunch of designs for brochures and T-shirts as well as some designs for Judy's old plant nursery employer. We limped along financially through moderate sales of the health drink networking, unemployment benefits, Judy's salary and my attempts at graphics, but it just wasn't enough to cover all of our expenses. Thanksgiving and Christmas loomed ahead and Judy's dad was due to arrive for his annual visit in a month or so. The apartment complex we were living in was pretty swift about giving their three-day 'quit' notice if the rent wasn't paid within the five day grace period and sure enough there was another one on my door again. My son Kurt had left a small leather bound New Testament Bible with us a year or so before which we had left on top of a bookcase collecting dust. Sitting all alone early one Monday morning I picked it up out of sheer curiosity and looked at it with my normal thoughts of "what the hell was my son thinking!"

I am Jewish, what would I ever need anything like that for much less reading any of it?

I was a heavy smoker for years. Three packs a day was not unusual for me at all to consume. My favorite brand was **More**. Someone told me later in life that More cigarettes were the worst brand you could smoke and there was a sign at a medical Clinic that said **'Don't smoke...and if you must smoke...don't smoke More's...and if you must smoke More's...don't smoke More Menthol'!** Well, there I was doing just that. I was so hooked that if I managed to get out of bed in the morning without lighting up and actually made it into the bathroom first, I was doing pretty good I hardly used matches or lighters...one butt lit up another! The sun rays were shining through the blinds and I could see all the smoke floating through the air as I decided to read the little New Testament in front of me. I sat each day, Monday to Friday reading one chapter each day. *"What in the world is all this Christianity about?"* I thought. The book chapters of Mark, Matthew, Luke and John were all the same story...with different perspectives. I did like the book of Acts; it was kind of like a novel. I had had it at that point though. Disgusted with my life and tired of working alone, I slammed the little Bible down on the table and looked up and yelled**... "If you're real, God, then show me!"** Walking slowly into our small galley style kitchen area, I lit up a brand new smoke. More cigarettes looked like miniature cigars with their brown paper wrappings. They were also much longer than normal white cigarettes. As I was about to lift the cigarette to my mouth, I watched in amazement as my left arm started to rise from it's limp position and my left hand reached out to my right wrist, grasping it very tightly and holding it away from my face. The fingers on my hand holding the cigarette also clamped down hard on the cigarette at the same time.

"WHAT THE HELL IS HAPPENING TO ME?"

My mind raced back and forth with instant and frightening thoughts of my total loss of mind control. I found myself staring at the bizarre situation for what seemed like hours watching as the cigarette I couldn't let go of (or smoke), burned slowly towards my fingers. Well, I thought, maybe some men in white coats will barge into the apartment and take me to a funny farm! Naahhh, I was too strong minded for that and too much of a chicken to commit suicide or just drive off and disappear....besides , I loved my wife and family too much to even consider that lame way out. I was totally frozen in time. There seemed to be absolutely no answer to my situation. I looked dumbfounded at the cigarette still burning, now dangerously close to my fingers. The strange thing about it was that More cigarettes usually went out a lot when not continually being dragged on and had to be re-lit a lot but this one just kept burning down! *As I stared at it, I heard a 'still small voice' say...* "*Have one more puff and put it out*". I wasn't sure if the voice was actually inside me, or was it just my momentary paranoia? It sounded very verbal but, whatever it was, my fingers released the pressure on the burning butt and my left hand released its grip on my right wrist. I took the much needed puff and put it out; from that time on I didn't even think about smoking.....(whatever that was)! Feeling strangely at ease and more relaxed than I had felt in days, I left the apartment to meet with a client who had called earlier. For the next few weeks I found myself chewing on gum and toothpicks but really not having a clue as to why. I even started to look at folks who had lit cigarettes in their mouths and wondered what they were doing. Judy noticed my non-smoking and got real nervous. Over the years I had tried to kick the habit but each and every time I behaved like a bear. No one wanted to be around me for those first few terrifying days and weeks, but I was showing none of the usual displays of rude behavior so the subject just wasn't brought up much. Besides, I was confused, I thought I needed something in my mouth but didn't have any reason for it.

I was in a strange new world and everything seemed odd.

Somehow, Judy and I pretended that things were going to work out. We were after all, as they say 'cockeyed optimists' at heart. The years had flown by and it was almost Christmas of 1989 over 16 years since we met. Although we had come dangerously close to a second divorce for both of us a few times during this period, our deep love for each other and the memories of our passionate early romance had miraculously kept us together. Someone one told me that Evangelist Billy Graham was asked if he had actually ever considered divorce. I don't know if that was true but according to the source who told me that, Rev Billy answered jokingly.... "Divorce never....MURDER....a few times!" Many times over the years we could have easily related to that remark!

The phone rang abruptly disturbing my creative attempts on the drawing board. "STAN", my wife's voice on the other end sounded excited but somewhat nervous!

(Judy)

"Seton just called me and said that we were precisely in the right place to receive an abundance of wealth!" "Yeah!, soooo....heard all that before". "I know, I know but hon, I really think we should do what she's telling us to do". "What's that Jude?" "Ummmm, well here's the scary part. She's going to give us a private coaching class but it's going to cost!!" "COST? How much is cost?" "Now don't get negative, she wants $5,000 for the course". "$5,000! Oh, no problem babe...just write out a check!" "Well...it's $5,000 each!" "EACH? Are you crazy...I mean..is she crazy? Where would we ever be able to get our hands on $10,000 or even $5,000?" "Look Stan, we haven't been able to line up with the universe perfectly yet but why not try? Let's just line up, ask around and see what happens?" "O.k. Jude, guess that's worth a try huh?"

(Stan)

Call after call was made without success. Seton was in constant contact with us telling us not to give up, that we were within fractions of perfect alignment with the universe and that finances were within our grasp. Unbelievably a $7,000 Bank Loan I had applied for the previous month to assist my fledgling graphics business had been approved. "What do you think Jude?, should we use some of the money to give to Seton? I mean, it doesn't look very promising to be getting it from anywhere else!" "You know Stan, either we can line up with the cash flow the way Seton says or forget it. If we use it for anything else but your business, then let's at least pay off some of our bills and a few small debts". "O.k. babe, sounds like a plan to me, that's the first smart decision we've made in a long time but let's not tell Seton anything just yet!"

Chapter 12

SET FREE
(Stan)

We barely heard the knock on the door of our apartment as we finished cleaning up the kitchen area and rehearsed the events of the day. "I'll get it Jude. Hi Barbara! What a surprise...c'mon in". Barbara was always a welcome sight and someone who always had a smile and a positive spirit in and around her. She seemed to be doing quite well with her multi-level business and was always seeking our advice on personal relationship. She had never been married and admired the obvious love and fun we almost always displayed. "If only I could find a man like you Stan", she would say quite often. "Oh yeah? Hey look Barb, there's a lot you don't know about me but thanks for the compliment" "I'll vouch for that", blurted Judy with a snickered laugh. "Heeey...watch it lady, I could tell Barb a few things about you too....hmmmm?" "O.K. you two, I didn't come here to start a fight". "Barb, see, that's what I mean by things you don't know about either of us...it's just our way of kidding around with each other....you haven't been around us in a real fight....it's not pretty!" Anyway, what brings you by tonight?" "Oh, I just enjoy your company and wanted to share some new benefits about our products with you. By the way, do you go to any particular church?" "CHURCH?" I almost spit out the coffee I had in my mouth as I started to drink it. "BARB! Didn't I tell you I was Jewish?" "Well yes, but I thought you might enjoy it.... it's not a 'typical' church." "Look Barb, I have nothing against churches but Judy and I are kind of 'free spirits' you know? We don't attend anything religious that way, only holidays and such. And besides, Judy's been to so many different churches she doesn't have a clue to what she is. We believe in a 'higher spirit' that's about it!" "O.k., O.k., I got it.....but you both might want to come to this 'church'...it's really fun....you might enjoy it". "O.K. Barb, stop bending my arm, its beginning to hurt.....we'll join you for laughs, what's the name of this fun filled? Church?" "Uhhh...it's called the *Church of the Inner Light.*"

"OOOHHH-KAAAYY....*Church of the Inner Light* huh? Ooooooo....sounds soooo intriguing" "Look you guys, come this Sunday, I'd just like having you both with me; you'll like Mike our pastor, she's a real hoot!" "SHE?, what d'ya mean SHE!....Your pastor is a woman?....then what is she a 'pastor-ette?" "Yes...so what? Is there some kind of law against that?" "No...It's just that I've always thought a pastor is supposed to be a man". "Well, look just come, see what it's like, you don't have go there again if you don't like it. I gotta go now,.call me if you're coming, I'll save your seats next to me".

"Wow Jude, Barb is such a hot ticket isn't she? Ya think we should go with her this Sunday?" "Stan, I think it would be fun like she said, you know, 'Inner Light' sounds so interesting, I'd like to go and see what's it's like, wouldn't hurt us to find out, we've been to just about everything else right?" "Yeah maybe, but a church is still a church isn't it? I mean...if they start in with a Jesus thing, I don't know but if they do...I won't say his name, I'm Jewish!" "Oh Jewish, Shmewish Stan, would you cut it out already... c'mon you're about as Jewish as I am a Christian. We've never been part of either religion in any serious way since we've met. Let's just go and meet some new folks and do something different". "All right babe, but just remember, I won't speak his name!" "O.k., O.k., if it will make you feel better, I won't either; stop making such a big deal over it, nobody else will know whether you do or don't and besides....that may not even be any issue anyway". "You're right hon, let's just go and humor Barbara....we can always join her for lunch afterwards. Be an interesting day that's for sure!" "Wow! It will be December 3rd already, what happened to this year?" "I don't know sweetheart, but I'm glad this year's over. It's been real and it's been interesting....but it hasn't been real interesting!" "You're right about that Stan, it's been a real bummer like a lot of other years.....when's this rollercoaster ride gonna stop?"

"I can't even think straight anymore"

(Judy)

Our life is such a whirlwind, I feel like I'm a puppet and someone is pulling the strings. Where are we going in life? I felt myself in a place I've never known or been in before. There were days I woke up and was so hungry for some answers. I was the kind of person that kept many thoughts and fears bottled up inside. As a child I had no one to talk to about my fears. I couldn't talk to my mother, she had her own problems and a child was seen but not heard back then as we were told. I can't express how my fears were grabbing hard at my gut. My dad was always happy; he loved so much of life. I worked hard at pretending with him and my brother. I was so afraid of disappointing either of them, they were my idols. Neither of them knew my real fears, I hid them well.

(Now....I'm in unfamiliar territory again not sure of what road to take!)

Seton keeps pressuring us for money and lining up with the universe. I can't seem to line up because the universe keeps moving and so does the money. Can't seem to connect with either of them! I'm so confused. Seton seems so strong and demanding and I'm fearful of demanding people, they represent total authority to me!

Stan, what do you think about what Barbara said? I remember the time back in New England when I saw this little church at Christmas with all the lights and I looked at you and just sighed *"Oh...chuurchhh"*. I remembered my childhood and teenage years when I went to church and the peace I felt. I never really understood it though., I just thought it was a place to escape to. I went to church here in California with Holly a few times but you always slept late to 12 o'clock, waking up just as we were coming home. Hey, we even went to a few services at a Temple with you but we let it all go. Did you really mean what you said that you might go to Barbara's church?" "Sure, why not? let's go and humor Barb like I said, what the heck, we've tried just about everything else!"

(Stan)

"You know Jude, Barb's pastor sure is a fascinating woman isn't she? I mean, everything Seton has been talking about, Pastor Mike says about the same thing only she quotes Scriptures from the Bible". "Well, you made it through the service without speaking Jesus name out loud; I was looking at you a lot". "Yeah, I didn't but somehow I wasn't even thinking about that; Mike was so interesting to listen to. I asked Barbara about the name of the church, you know...*Church of the Inner light*...and she said it used to be a 'New Age Church' .but Pastor Mike got 'born again', whatever that means, and turned it into a Christian Fellowship". "Hmmm...I don't really know much about New Age stuff...except for what Seton talks about, but there's a lot of similarity to it and Christianity don't you think?" "Well, kind of I guess, they both sound so positive but Seton's always into lining up with 'The Universe'. Mike stuck to what she called the Word of God. Look, I even bought a tape of the service; I want to hear what Mike said again, my mind was off in a million different directions but I wasn't bored that's for sure". "So, think we should go back again next week? I feel a lot more relaxed now and you look a lot more at ease too!" "Yeah, why not, what could it hurt? I'm getting real tired of not being able to 'line up with the universe', whatever that's all about and Seton's still at me about letting the cash flow in so we can take her private coaching".

(Judy)

Stan seems different since he stopped smoking. He doesn't even remember smoking? He kept talking about an encounter with God but he's not even sure about that! Actually we're still having a hard time trying to grasp all of this. It's like he was 'delivered' from the habit and still doesn't know he had a habit. It's all so weird but I watch him so peaceful and relaxed I'd like to have that experience 'cause I'm still struggling to quit smoking myself. I kept watching him waiting to see if he would give in and start up again but he never did. Three packs a day and now nothing!

"Stan, do you think that God would do that for me?" "Hey hon, I don't know if that whole experience was God or what.....although I did ask him to show me if he was real...who knows? All I know is that I don't remember smoking but it should make it easier for you to quit being around me now! You know, I can hardly even talk to you about it. I have absolutely no memory of EVER smoking or what it feels like after that day in the kitchen...can you understand that?" "No, I guess not. I can't get my brain to wrap around that at all". "Me either....when my left hand grabbed my right wrist I thought I was losing it!"

(Stan)

"SHE SAID WHAT? ...Jude, honey, stop crying......say that again!" "STAN, I was just talking to her on the phone at work today. Seton said that because we paid our bills instead of paying her that you were cursed and that you'd never get another job!" "CURSED!....why that two faced bitch, boy, she sure showed her true colors didn't she? Hey, that does it babe, we're through with her and she's been giving me the creeps lately anyway. Didn't I see a notice in Pastor Mike's bulletin about some mid week classes she's giving....I mean, a lot of the sessions look just like Seton's subject matter but Mike's only charging $50 a person. That's a lot less than the $10,000 or even $5,000 Seton wanted". "Oh...O.k. Stan, I thought you'd be upset, I feel better now" "UPSET? are you kidding, that two faced witch can take a hike, what business was it of her's to tell you anything like that especially knowing you were at work! She better be prepared for me soon, I'll get right in that pudgy little face of her's and let her have it!" "STAN, STAN...let it go, I'm alright now that we've talked. She just shocked me. She was really angry on the phone; I wasn't prepared to hear her talk like that ever". "You know hon; I listened to Pastor Mike's tape several times. She really *'speaks to me'* in a way I've never heard before. And you know, it's amazing I can hear, I mean...I've never really been able to react well to women in authority. Guess that stems from my mother. She was a real sweetheart, beautiful and very generous, but she was always the loudest voice in the house; she was like the ruler there. My dad was pretty much a 'woos', if you know what I mean. I loved him and he was the financial brains but my mother was the one in charge, she could get real over bearing sometimes. We were constantly butting heads as I grew up, but there's something about Mike that I respect. She even wears those high heels on the stage. I had to keep myself from chuckling a few times hearing the click, click, click of those heels on the wooden stage as she walked back and forth. But, she does look good...I'll give her that. Her husband Chuck is really quiet huh?" "Yes, he's such a nice guy isn't he?" "Yeah, I guess he's more in charge of the administration. They remind me a lot of my parents that way but somehow I feel O.k. with it you know!"

(Judy)

I decided to go out to the pool and try to write my book. I had put it away because I felt that I had writer's block and maybe I could start again. There were so many thoughts racing through my mind. This new church was so intriguing, our New Age guru Seton., my whole life in general. As I sat quietly thinking about the 'spirit guides' who helped me write *'Frenchtown Lady'*, nothing more was coming up to me; 24 chapters and now absolutely nothing? I felt that I was jumping into a new dimension or something. *"My goodness, what's happening to me? What happened to my spirit guides?"* I know that psychic said I would have a best seller, .or was that all real? As I sat by the pool I picked up the book and started to read some pages. Wow! How was all this put on paper, 24 chapters worth and now nothing! Stan was pressuring me to finish but something was stopping me. I had no answers but I knew an answer was there but I wasn't ready to hear it yet. I jumped in the pool to clear my head and to try to break free from so many thoughts clogging my brain. I heard myself crying inside.

"Oh God, I need some answers now!"
(Maybe He could help. I tried everything and everyone else! All of sudden I felt at peace. It felt comforting to just relax, put the book down and rest!)

I thought, yeah there are a lot of writers who go through this. As I walked back to our apartment, I walked in and explained to Stan how I was feeling. I wasn't sure of his reaction; he just wanted this book done. He had designed the cover of it, edited it, typed it and had done a really great job with it. "O.k. babe, I knew that you weren't going to come back with any more written". "How did you know that Stan?" "Oh...I just did! I had a feeling inside, let's just put the book down until it's time". We were both very confused two years of work, near the end and the words are not flowing. I felt sad but still at a strange peace.

"Stan...it's Tuesday night, Barbara called and wants us to join the class at the church. It's $50 each, do you want to go?" "Why not...sure beats the $10,000 Seton is charging". The first night we got to know a lot of new folks and Pastor Mike was a great speaker as usual. I loved the people at the class, they were so much fun. We still had no idea why we were there but we trusted Barbara and it worked out really good. Seton wasn't giving up. She kept calling and trying to get us to *line up with the universe* and come to her class. I made a mistake once by asking my brother Bob for some cash and he came through but we paid a psychic instead of our bills. I wasn't raised to lie but the life path I was choosing to follow was pulling on me hard. Christmas was fast approaching, my dad was flying in from Florida and I put everything on hold. I wanted to get ready for the holidays. Stan and I were struggling a lot with our finances then and we even had a three day 'quit notice' on our door, but he managed to work the rent out with the management. Dad always gave us money at Christmas so we knew that we could pay it, at least for that month anyway! I never wanted my dad to know our financial state. He had worked hard all his life for everything and I didn't want him to think less of us.

The day came for his arrival. We watched anxiously at the airport for his all too familiar attire. "Oh my God Stan, look...there he is!" We both began to chuckle. He was quite a character. Here he was again, his yearly visit; still 6 feet tall, a little bow legged and wearing a cowboy hat, orange socks, tennis shoes, checkered pants and a striped shirt. None of the colors matched at all, in fact all of the colors clashed! "HEY BUNNY", (his favorite nickname for me) he yelled as he came struttin' over to us. "Like my new hat? I figured if I'm going west I should look like a westerner". "Well dad, you sure look different". We all had a laugh over his looks; he was so much fun that he made you forget all your troubles. "Hey Dad, a friend of ours who I want you to meet wants us to go to a service at her church Wednesday night. It's getting near Christmas so we thought it would be fun. Holly's going to come with us too". "Oh sure...I'll go talk to Buster" (the name dad called God by). He was always looking up saying..."So Buster...what's up?" We loved his sense of humor. "Stan, look how beautiful the church is decorated. I just love Christmas, it's such a happy time of year". "Well, I'm learning Jude. I always envied my Christian friends and wanted to be part of the holiday. People all seemed to be happy; buying gifts, which my family being Jewish liked a lot. They gave their employees a lot of extras.

It was fun singing Christmas songs and even Stan was singing along. The words were put up on a screen. Pastor Mike really poured her heart out in the sermon. We all loved it. Near the end of the service she asked everyone to stand and to receive Jesus as their personal Savior. I was shocked to see Stan standing next to me as well as Holly and my dad. I almost laughed out loud as I heard my dad say (as he turned back looking at his chair)....."Whoa, did someone put a spring in my seat?". He wasn't very quiet about it but no-one else seemed to hear him. As we verbally asked Jesus to come into our heart, I couldn't believe my ears. Stan was also doing the same with tears rolling down his face. The end of the service came and Pastor Mike made an announcement. "You know, for many years this has been a New Age Church. A few months ago, after I received new life in Christ through an evangelistic TV Network program, I renounced New Age and changed the church into a Christian fellowship. I guess a lot of my congregation objected and ran but you are the chosen ones who have stayed on. I've decided that "The Church of 'The Inner Light' is not an appropriate name anymore.

From this day on, it is now called
"Community Church of God's Word"

We returned home that day, with a new excitement and a new hope for our future. Somehow we had finally been able to **'Reach Through The VEIL of Deceit'** which had blinded the eyes of our heart and had caused us so much pain and suffering over the years. Stan's boys were not very happy about their father's new faith, but he could not return to the 'void' which had such a negative hold on him all his life. JUDY did you hear what Pastor Mike and her associate pastor said when they prayed with us!" "Oh...you mean about Seton?" "Yeah, that and other things, but they knew her personally when they were a New Age church and didn't want to manipulate us in any way so they were praying for us ever since they found out about Seton that we would find out the truth and get away from her teaching and that class she wanted us to join for $5,000". "Well it worked babe, I feel so relieved about not having to *'line up with the universe'* but mostly about finding out that there really is a living God who wants the best for us. I guess bumping into that dark negative spiritual world we were involved with was the reality that there's actually a real spiritual battle going on. Thank God He is alive and well and has defeated all of that. All we had to do was to believe, right?" "Right hon, but so many years we endured all those lies from the pit of hell...what a waste!" "Naah Stan....not a waste...just a learning curve and at least we learned in time to enjoy a lot of more years together. How do you feel about receiving Jesus...I mean...you've always been so determined about not even saying his name...or....do you just call Him by His Hebrew name Yeshua?"..Oh..Jesus..Yeshua, what matters is that I have a personal relationship with a living God. I can actually talk to Him and He talks with me in lots of different ways. It's amazing Jude, I'm learning more about being Jewish as a Christian than I did as a Jew...I mean...the Old Testament Torah and the New Testament comes alive when I read it all now! I'm definitely not a Jew who loves Jesus....I'm a Christian who loves Jews....and all humans no matter!"

WOW, what a different experience for the four of us. We felt like new babies just experiencing life in such a different way. We loved going to happy hours for a little snack and drink after work but one of those days there was a bachelor party at the bar but when the strippers appeared it felt real funny.

"Honey, let's go, I'm not comfortable". As I said the words, they seemed strange but they also felt the right thing to say. As time went on we wanted to tell the world about our new found faith but many walked away from us just as we did for so many years. We were so hungry to know all about Jesus. We studied, we read, took classes. I thought back to the time when I was a little girl and all the things I heard. I tried to combine what I remembered to my new found teaching. Pastor Mike was only six months ahead of us and we all went by her leading. I began to walk in fear. Oh my, God was not going to love me if I didn't read my Bible, pray or go to church....even dance (which was my passion). I put myself under such condemnation. I felt guilty all the time. My fears began manifesting into my newly found faith. Stan had no religiosity being Jewish. He saw my stress and heard my lectures. "We didn't pray long enough today Stan" or "we didn't read the Bible at 8 o'clock when we said we would". Stan went along with me for a while until one day he had enough. "Judy", he said lovingly but sternly, "I became a Christian to have a peaceful life, not to have to keep up with trying to work all the laws of Judaism and now you are saying if we don't do this or don't do that then Jesus won't bless us?"

Stan grabbed the Word and showed me in John 14:17 how much God loves us no matter what we do. Jesus doesn't put rules or regulations on us or beat us up. He gives us all choices. The one thing He wants from us is our heart and to let Him love us. It took me a long time to be honest with you readers...actually, it took years until finally one day I heard a preacher say that Jesus loves us unconditionally but religion puts us in bondage. Jesus is interested only in a personal relationship. He wants to be your friend.

Whoa...that really hit home! I felt so set free, I'm not going to hide in a bubble and beat myself up or slap myself just because I still do the things I always loved....like dancing! I get angry at man for trying to put rules on people. Your heart just won't let you do sinful things and if you do mess up...so what? Ask Him for forgiveness and move on.

"WOW, WOW, WOW...Stan....did you hear that pastor last night? Just have a personal relationship with God. I can talk to Him like a friend anytime, anywhere! I'm not perfect that's for sure (even though I thought I was....just kidding!)....and He is here to love me". "Yep Jude, you finally got it".

Stan decided to go to a Bible study and I decided to stay home. As I sat on the couch just talking to my new friend I found myself asking Him what he wanted me to do with a 24 chapter book I was writing. It only took a minute and I heard His still small voice inside me say...."Rip it up". Rip it up? I looked around and thought.. "That can't be God" It took two years to write. "Hello? God? Was that you telling me to rip it up?" I heard Him again. "Rip the book up". "But why God" I said quietly in shock. "Because it doesn't edify ME". I began to cry. I don't know if I cried because of two years of work gone or knowing what was in that book and how it was written. I walked slowly into the bedroom and grabbed the book which I had hidden under the bed and just cried and cried. Yes, I could have kept the book and ignored what I knew I had heard but I had a choice to make. He knows our past, present and future and I know I would have slipped back into 'darkness', edifying psychics, tarot cards and all the ugly darkness that goes along with it. I waited impatiently for Stan to come home to tell him. "What do you think honey?" Stan wasn't that surprised but still a little shocked by my words. "Well...we both know why it has to go but do you think we can at least keep the cover I designed? It was so perfect for the title of 'Frenchtown Lady'. "STAN, it ALL goes!" We both felt a release and knew that someday the book would be re-written the way it should be to tell the world about the dark side of deception.

Now is that time reader and you have been reading the new version

Spirits Exposed
Chapter 13

Authors' Note:

To you who have shared our travels through happy times, hellish times, times of despair, confusion and "shaking", we invite you to continue on. **Chapter 12,"Set Free"** is not the end of our story here on this planet.

Chapter 13, **"Spirits Exposed"** *is the very reason for the writing of this book and is illustrated for your enlightenment and protection from the reality of a 'spiritual realm' which conceals itself in seemingly harmless forms. Yes, many situations which happen to us all stem a lot from our own un-wise decisions however, many of those same decisions have been influenced by unseen spirits as will be explained. Hopefully, the "eyes of your understanding" will embrace the truth set forward in the pages to follow and you will be able to avoid the pitfalls that lie in wait to ambush the uniformed.*

SPIRITS EXPOSED

(Stan)

Dear Reader: For what it's worth, many areas of this book were very difficult for us to re-live and write about. The one and only benefit of our 'negative' spiritual involvements over our yearly emotional and financial rollercoaster ride was to find out that a positive spiritual realm and reality really does exist. His name is Father God. He exists in three forms but all the same substance such as water, ice and steam. God the Father is **"His Heart"**. Jesus, His Son, is **"His Word"**. The Holy Spirit is **"His Hands"** doing His work through us here on planet earth. The triune God is of course a lot more complicated than that, but all we humans need to understand is that it is the simplest and most direct way of explaining a God who is very much alive and loves everything about humans and the world we live in. He alone created all of it and all of us no matter what we look like, no matter where we live. What it takes to truly appreciate Him is to understand His 'unconditional' love for humanity and His heart's desire for all of us to have happy, healthy and prosperous lives as well as all of the 120 years he has allotted for each of us. (**Genesis 6:3**). Do we all inherit this life and do we all live out our years to this degree? The answer is obviously NO, but then He also gives us the ability to 'choose' what we believe, what we eat, how we live, what we get involved in and who we get involved with. God is not the author of trauma, disease, poverty, anger, depression or anything else we humans 'allow' into our lives. Any one of these can and will alter His plans for us. His only title is love. He has a purpose for every person and we have to find out our purpose for being here. We are the ones who 'allow' demonic spirits to invade our thought patterns and 'deceive' us in our thinking and our actions. Lucifer, who was actually the original Praise and Worship leader in Heaven before humanity existed, challenged God and fell from heaven with one third of all of the angels who followed him. He became Satan and his kingdom was finally destroyed by Jesus.

He and his angels, however, are still ever present and capable of antagonizing humans, imitating and even appearing as those who have passed away. 'Paranormal' activities can materialize as the '*dearly departed*' as well as all of the other hundreds of belief systems in this world of ours such as 'reincarnation' and the like and are routinely voiced through those known as 'Psychics'. The Bible clearly states that "to be absent from the body is to be present with the Lord" (**2 Corinthians 5:8**). The dead cannot and do not float around in space nor come back (or be brought back) for a visit at any time. The "voices" Psychics hear and the 'spirits' they 'see' are actually the 'fallen angels' of Satan himself! The only real 'truth' and key to an understanding and full comprehension of the Bible is believing in one's heart and speaking out loud from one's mouth that Jesus was crucified for our sins and our iniquities and was raised from the dead on the third day and is now sitting at the right hand of Father God. Only then, will anyone achieve New Life in Christ and only an 'intimate vertical relationship' with a living God can achieve a life of peace beyond all human understanding and a deeper conscious 'hearing' of His 'still small voice', circumstances, feelings, signs, wonders, etc. within us. We urge anyone reading our book to turn this page and to recite the prayer on it. There are also many scriptures listed which you are encouraged to look up in the Bible no matter what version of the Bible you have or come across. You are also encouraged to join a faith filled, energetic Word of Life church so that you can fellowship with like believers for strength and agreement in prayer for your needs. If you are, per chance, a psychic, clairvoyant, soothsayer or metaphysics follower, we urge you especially to forsake your god(s) and follow Jesus before it's too late to live in eternity with God in heaven. You especially were given a gift of Prophecy but that gift has been perverted. We are, after all, living, speaking spirits ourselves. We have a soul (mind, will and emotions) and we live in a temporary 'tent' we call a body. We will all live on somewhere after the body dies. God wishes that **ALL would become the image of his son (Romans 8:29**) and live in the abundance of SHALOM he has prepared for us. Shalom in Hebrew meaning 'peace', *everything perfect, nothing missing nothing lacking*".

We would hope that in the reading of our experiences, that in some dramatic way you will open the '*eyes of your understanding*' and the "hearing" of your HearT and will be able to avoid the pitfalls and consequences of **"The VEIL Of Deceit"** which saturates almost everything you hear and see on TV, movies, the internet as well as from misinformed and misled educational teachers, politicians and even close friends and family members. Think clearly and make every attempt to listen to the only true advice coming from the only truth there is. Jehovah, Jesus, Yeshua, the Alpha and the Omega, Father God, the Ancient of Days, 'Buster'. or. whatever name you feel comfortable 'relating' to him may be. Do not get caught up in 'religion' or 'religious doctrines' which put a wall up between you and Him. Your personal relationship with God is yours alone. Talk with Him daily and get to know Him. He knows everything about you. He knew you before the foundations of the earth were even created. He knows how many hairs you have on your head. You can tell Him your deepest thoughts and your deepest concerns. He alone will become your best friend and the only friend who cannot hide the truth from you because....**HE IS TRUTH! The Truth is, we have all sinned and deserve God's judgment. God, the Father,** sent **His only son (Jesus Christ)** <u>to satisfy that judgment for those who believe on Him</u>. Jesus, is the creator of all and eternal Son of God. He lived a totally **sinless life**, and He loved us so much that He died for our sins, taking the punishment that we deserve, was buried and rose from the dead according to the Bible. If you truly believe and trust this in your heart, receiving Jesus alone as your Savior, declaring, **"Jesus is Lord"** you will be saved from judgment and spend eternity with God in heaven

NEW LIFE IN CHRIST

To receive New Life in Christ, please recite this simple prayer

"Father, I know that I have broken your laws and my sins have separated me from you. I am truly sorry, and now I want to turn away from my past sinful life toward you. Please forgive me and help me avoid sinning again. I believe that your son, Jesus Christ died for my sins, was resurrected from the dead, is alive and hears my prayer. I invite Jesus to become Lord of my life, to rule and reign in my heart from this day forward. Please send your Holy Spirit help me obey you and do your will for the rest of my life. In Jesus name I pray, Amen."

NUEVA VIDA EN CRISTO

Para recibir nueva vida en Cristo, recita por favor esta sencilla oración.

Padre Santo, yo se que he roto tus leyes y mis pecados me han separado de ti. Estoy sinceramente arrepentido, ahora quiero alejarme de mi vida pecadora y acercarme a ti. Perdóname por favor y ayúdame a no pecar otra vez. Creo que tu hijo Jesucristo murió por mis pecados, resucitó de entre los muertos, esta vivo y escucha mi oración. Invito a Jesús para que sea el Señor de mi vida, para gobernar y reinar en mi corazón desde este día en adelante. Envía por favor tu Santo Espíritu, ayúdame a obedecer y hacer tu voluntad por el resto de mi vida. En el nombre de Jesús te lo pido. Amén

There was war in heaven: Michael and his angels fought against the Dragon; and the Dragon and his angels fought, and prevailed not; neither was their place found any more in heaven. And the great Dragon was cast out, that old serpent, called the Devil, and Satan, which **deceiveth** the whole world:

Revelation 12:7-9

HE WAS CAST OUT INTO THE EARTH, AND HIS ANGELS WERE CAST OUT WITH HIM.

These are the same "unclean spirits" that Jesus cast out of so many "possessed" souls as He walked the length and breadth of ancient Judea. Following their attempt to depose God from His throne in heaven in the beginning, they were cast back down to the earth and have been in a condition of "restraint" since... awaiting Judgment Day. It's more than evident that they still have a certain amount of interface with man ... but not quite enough to do what they would like to with "God's special creation" - utterly destroy it.

Angels are 'spirit beings'…spirits don't die.
The spirits that Jesus cast out
during His earthly ministry
ARE STILL AROUND TODAY!

Final comments from the authors:

(Stan)

Well Judy, as Jesus said on the cross, "It is finished". He achieved for mankind what none of us could ever do and I believe that He wrote this book through us out of His deep desire to free all of us from being gypped out of the life of goodness, hope and promise that He died for.

(Judy)
As His word says in **Romans 8:1**
"There is now NO condemnation in Christ Jesus"

*Yes Stan. I truly hope and pray that everyone who has read our story and has taken the challenge to receive Jesus as Lord and Savior, if they hadn't done so already, will be more aware than ever of the **"deceit"** which can come in so many seemingly innocent ways and which can totally manipulate the purpose intended for our lives by God. Many might say "but see, your purpose was to experience what you wrote about in order to testify to the truth!". The real TRUTH here is, God knows exactly what our choices will be in life as He does yours (the reader)....and He may use those choices for His Glory...but He definitely will not use the devil or his angels to confuse us or cause us any harm.*

We hope you've been blessed by our story. Life is supposed to be joyous even with all of our trials, tears and hardships.

But there's someone now we can lean on and He is always there to carry us through.

John 3:16
"For God so loved the world that he gave his one and only son, that whoever believes in him shall not perish but have eternal life

"The Beginning"

REACH THROUGH YOUR VEILS OF DECEIT AND LIVE FREE"
Email: PrayersAnswered @theveilofdeceit.com

Made in the USA
Charleston, SC
25 April 2012